Ethics.
A Quick Immersion

Michael Slote

ETHICS
A Quick Immersion

Tibidabo Publishing
New York

Published by Tibidabo Publishing, Inc. New York.

Copyediting by Lori Gerson
Cover art by Raimon Guirado

First published: November 2023

Visit our Series on our Web:
www.quickimmersions.com

ISBN: 978-1-949845-36-5
1 2 3 4 5 6 7 8 9 10

Library of Congress Control Number: 2023949580

Printed in the United States of America.

Contents

Chapter 1

Introduction

This book is part of a series devoted to making one or another area of specialized thought accessible to educated intelligent readers who have no prior acquaintance with the given area. The area of the present book is the discipline of ethics, and I use the term "discipline" because, of course, we all talk about ethics outside any such specialization. We deplore someone's ethics, call someone unethical, talk about "professional ethics," and so on. Further too, the specialization called ethics deals with moral questions and is sometimes equated with the idea of "moral philosophy," and of course again non-specialists speak about morality all the time—as when we speak of right and wrong, where the word "morally" is implicitly understood. But still, moral philosophy and ethics (the latter notion is for various reasons a bit broader) aren't being done in a formal or systematic way when non-specialists speak in the above ways, and I want to introduce you to ethics as a specialized field or discipline, one that is relevant to much else in life but has its own internal concepts and issues.

Ethics in this sense can, however, be divided into three parts: normative ethics, metaethics, and applied ethics, and let me briefly explain this subdivision. Normative ethics seeks to give us an understanding of what is right or wrong, good or bad, rational or irrational. The issues that arise in this connection are diverse and complex, and humankind has been doing ethics in this sense for more than two thousand years. Metaethics is a more recent development. It asks what we semantically mean when we say that something is right or wrong or good or bad. It also asks whether some interpretations of ethical vocabulary undermine the possibility of ethical knowledge and even ethical truth. Applied ethics typically seeks to apply one or another form of normative ethics to practical contemporary questions like: when is abortion permissible? Is capital punishment morally acceptable? What do the richer nations owe to the poorer ones? Many professors in philosophy departments work in metaethics or applied ethics (or both), but by far the greatest emphasis among philosophers is and always has been normative ethics, and this book will mainly focus on this discipline.

However, it will do that in a way that I believe is without precedent and much to your (the reader's) advantage. I said that ethics as part of philosophy more generally has been done for more than two thousand years, but every historical-cum-disciplinary book about ethics I have ever heard of limits its attention to a single one of the main traditions of ethics, formal ethics, that have sprung up on this planet. Philosophy has originated endogenously in only three human cultures: the Indian, the Chinese, and the Greece-based Western. But there is no book seeking to introduce all three of these traditions and certainly no book that attempts to show to readers how the three might work to enrich one another. The traditions have gone forward mainly in isolation from one another, but we live in an increasingly internationalized world, and it is my belief, exhibited in what follows, that any good introduction to ethics has to take the three main traditions of ethics seriously and show how they might interact with one another in a way that would benefit the field of ethics as a whole. (By way of parenthesis, let me just briefly explain why I limit philosophy to three main endogenous traditions. Japanese and Korean philosophy develop partly from the Chinese; and ancient Israel, Egypt, and Babylonia had nothing we can call philosophy.)

In the late twentieth century the Chinese philosopher Feng Qi coined the notion of *world philosophy* to apply to work that seeks to critically integrate different main philosophical traditions, and following that usage, we can say that the present book seeks to give an account of *world ethics.* In order to acquaint you with the main issues of ethics, I shall have to give you a bit of the historical background of certain normative ethical ideas and problems, but the latter will be what mainly occupies us. Let's proceed.

Moral notions/concepts lie at the heart of normative ethics. Those notions are to a large extent held in common by the three endogenous philosophical traditions I mentioned above, and they most centrally or fundamentally include the ideas of moral wrongness, moral obligation, and moral goodness. Other ideas come in as important to ethics or moral philosophy insofar as they seem highly relevant to the concepts just mentioned. Respect is an important moral idea because we think it is wrong to treat someone with disrespect; justice is important because only a just society can in moral terms be a good one; sympathy and empathy are important because they are part of the psychology of a morally good or virtuous person; reason or rationality is important because only rational beings can understand that they are under a moral obligation; and I could go further with other concepts that are going to be in play later in our discussion. But perhaps the most important ethical concept that historically and actually gets related to questions of morality is the concept of human well-being or welfare, or of a good life.

Almost every moral philosophy thinks we have some sort of obligation to contribute to the well-being of others, even if it is only to save them from harm if we can readily do so. Harm is deeply connected with the idea of well-being/welfare, as are also concepts like hurting, pain, happiness, tragedy, and disaster. So all these concepts are treated by philosophers as relevant to the doing of ethics.

I above mentioned sympathy and rationality as relevant to ethics, but *the contrast between them* is perhaps the main axis of ethics as a theoretical discipline. Many Western moral philosophers think that it is through reason or rationality that we come to know moral truths like "it is wrong to hurt babies" and "it is wrong to make a false promise." (When the American "Declaration of Independence" says "we hold these truths to be self-evident," it is saying that reason can by itself come to know them.) These same philosophers, known as *ethical rationalists*, also hold that the apprehension of moral truth can and should motivate us to act accordingly. If we really know via reason that it is wrong to make false (lying) promises, then we will be accordingly motivated to avoid doing so (except when we have "weak wills").

Ethical rationalism has been a major player in the historical development and present-day practicing of moral philosophy, but there has also been some major opposition to it on the part of philosophers who are called "moral sentimentalists." (For some reason they are not called "ethical sentimentalists.")

These philosophers hold that our understanding of moral norms requires us to have sympathy/empathy for others and that reason is either irrelevant to or insufficient for this goal. They also think that it makes no sense to suppose reason can motivate action or desire, but that sympathy *can* motivate us to act rightly or even admirably.

Interestingly enough, no Chinese or Indian philosopher has ever sided with the rationalists. They all think emotion/feeling has a necessary role in moral knowledge, moral action, and the moral life more generally. It is only in the West that we get ethical rationalism as I have described it, but here it has and has had a great influence on many philosophers who have theorized about ethics. The axis of rationalism/sentimentalism will constitute perhaps the main axis of the quick immersion I am offering you into ethics. But before I launch further in that direction let me introduce you to two important ethical theses that to a large extent lie to one side of the just-mentioned axis: hedonism and psychological egoism.

In ordinary English (and I assume the same goes for Spanish) "hedonism" is the name we give to the exclusive or impulsive individual pursuit of pleasure. But in philosophy it has a different but related meaning; it is the thesis that only pleasure or happiness in and of itself makes our lives go better. If money or hard work enable us to enjoy our lives more, they make our lives go better, but according to hedonism they only do so because they increase our overall pleasure or happiness. From what I have just said, hedonism may seem an obvious truth to many of you readers, but it is also possible to come up with reasons why hedonism may not be correct. We say "it is better to have loved and lost than never to have loved at all," and in saying this we typically *don't suppose* that a lovelorn life is more pleasant or happier than one where love never entered the picture. To that extent, love may not be a hedonic good, and neither, for similar reasons, do we have to think that accomplishment and even wisdom automatically make for greater happiness. Yet, as with love, it is possible to think of such things as contributing to a good or better life, and this then constitutes further reason to have doubts about the thesis of hedonism.

Psychological egoism is another thesis that has been defended and adopted by some philosophers. It holds that everything we do or deliberately do is motivated by self-interest, by a desire to advance our own well-being as much as possible. We can be led in this direction if we focus on many charitable acts that have basically egoistic or selfish/self-interested motivation behind them: spending time doing charity work because that will look good on the resumé one is submitting for college admission. Then there is also a (notorious) argument that can lead one to mistakenly think psychological egoism *has to be* true. After all, when I spend time helping an old person who needs help, I act on a desire that is entirely my own, and isn't it selfish or self-interested if I am preoccupied with satisfying one of my own desires? But I will bet many of you readers, perhaps all of you, will recognize the sophism of the brief argument for psychological egoism I just stated. To be sure, the helping person acts on a desire of their own, but the *object* or *goal* of that desire is not their own welfare but that of another person. That intuitively makes the action altruistic, not egoistic. Later on, we shall also see how empathy works via or within altruistic motivation, but at this point let's proceed to the very central issue of rationalism vs. sentimentalism. To do with understandably and well, we will need to give some historical background.

As I mentioned earlier, there have been no ethical rationalists in China and India, even though some philosophers in those traditions have given rationality *a place* in their overall ethical thinking. In the West, though, rationalism has always been a major intellectual force. Plato, Aristotle, and the Stoics were rationalists, and in the world of modern philosophy, there have been many rationalists too, most prominent and influential among them the eighteenth-century German philosopher Immanuel Kant. In recent times, rationalism has flourished in the work of some very well-known and influential philosophers, among them T. M. Scanlon, Christine Korsgaard, and Thomas Nagel. (In an appendix to this book I will offer some references to these and other philosophers I shall be mentioning that may help those of you who are interested explore the ideas discussed here at greater length and with further implications and considerations.)

But now I need to tell you about another major ethical distinction that cuts across the opposition between ethical rationalism and moral sentimentalism. The rationalism of the ancient (Western) world approached the ethical realm in a very different way from the rationalism of modern and of recent times, and recognizing that requires that we make a new and important distinction between types of normative ethical theory. The rationalists of the ancient world were all what is called virtue ethicists, and very few modern rationalists can be characterized in those terms.

To understand what virtue ethics is, we need to employ a temporal scheme of apparatus that derives from the work of the philosopher Jorge Garcia. According to his scheme, forms of normative ethics are distinguished by the way they relate the evaluation of acts to the time at which an action occurs. To take the simplest example, consider the utilitarian view that acts are to be morally assessed entirely in terms of their (likely) consequences. A given act is right if and only if it has good or optimal consequences for human happiness or well-being. This doctrine is in fact quite old. The Chinese philosopher Mozi espoused a form of utilitarianism more than 400 years before the Common Era, but in modern times utilitarian moral theory was mainly promulgated in England and then later throughout the English-speaking world. The main modern utilitarians were Jeremy Bentham, John Stuart Mill, and Henry Sidgwick, all English philosophers, but let me get back to Garcia's classificatory scheme.

On his view, the main difference among theories is whether they evaluate actions in terms of what comes later, what comes before they occur, or what holds when they occur. Utilitarianism of the most familiar variety and as we have seen classifies actions as right or wrong according to what comes later than those actions—either good consequences or bad or some mixture thereof. However, some utilitarians (Sidgwick) have been rationalists and others (Bentham) have not been.

But unlike utilitarians of whatever stripe, ancient rationalists evaluated actions in relation to the character or motivations that gave or could give rise to those actions. Moral assessment of actions depended on an assessment of the character or motives that came before or could give rise to them. The name for this kind of normative approach/ theory is *virtue ethics*, and all the rationalists of the ancient world—Plato, Aristotle, the Stoics—were virtue ethicists. They all held that the moral value of an action depends on questions about the kind of moral character that could or did give rise to that action. What exists *earlier* than an action is decisive to determining whether it is right or wrong.

Finally, then, there are normative approaches or theories that evaluate actions in terms of what exists *at the time of the actions*, and the most famous of modern ethical rationalists advocated this way of morally evaluating actions. Certain rationally understandable rules or principles constitute, for Kant, the standard one must appeal to in evaluating any action. If the act falls under some valid rule or principle, it is right; if not it is wrong. And the rules were said to hold at all times including the time a given action would occur. So the classifying scheme we get from Garcia cuts across the rationalism/sentimentalism distinction, and all three ways of relating actions to ongoing time can be realized in rationalist mode.

With sentimentalism, things are somewhat different. The Scottish philosopher David Hume is arguably the most important modern-day sentimentalist, and he largely grounded moral assessments in considerations about the consequences of action—his views helped bring about the later emergence of modern-day utilitarianism. But other sentimentalists are virtue ethicists. The ancient Chinese philosopher Mencius thought compassion and other such feelings were the basis of morality, and the evaluation of actions clearly depended for him on the nature of the motivation that underlies given actions and exists before they occur. Similarly, the nineteenth-century British moral philosopher James Martineau held that the moral character of an action depends on the feeling or emotion that lies behind the action, and this too combines sentimentalism with a virtue-ethical emphasis on evaluating actions in terms of what comes earlier. Garcia's scheme isn't, however, completely applicable to sentimentalist ethics. I know of no sentimentalist who has said we should evaluate actions in terms of some basic rule that holds valid at the time of the action and always. This lacuna may be due to the fact that basic rules are thought to be discernible only by reason, and sentimentalists would hold that such thinking makes too great a concession to the rationalist moral view of things. Given all the classificatory distinctions we have been making, it is time now to get down to some normative business.

Because Kant-type ethical rationalism is the most influential form of normative theorizing in academic circles nowadays, I want to begin by discussing ethical rationalism. If it offers in its own terms an adequate (and interesting) account of the normative, then we should be grateful to know about it, and perhaps sentimentalism wouldn't need to enter the picture at all—except perhaps as a historical coda. On the other hand, if, as I believe, there are some deep problems with the way rationalism approaches the realm of the ethical, then we might look to sentimentalism for a better way of ethically seeing things. It all depends on how good the arguments are on one side or the other.

But before I start talking about rationalism, there is one more issue I think I need to take up with you, an issue or question about the way I have been proceeding that may bother some, or many, of you. I have been talking about normative ethics as if moral philosophers were in search of moral truth and were simply disagreeing about where such truth lies or how it is best articulated. But this assumes or seems to assume that there is such a thing as moral truth, and some of you will come to this book a bit or more than a bit skeptical about whether there really can be such a thing. Now as I mentioned at the beginning of the book, the field of metaethics considers semantic questions about the nature of moral terminology that can lead one to doubt there can be such a thing as moral truth. One semantic view of moral vocabulary holds that when we say something is good, we are just expressing our positive feelings about it rather than making a significant judgment about it. On this view, which is called emotivism, "x is good" just means "hurrah for x," and the latter cannot be true or false. It just expresses an emotion. But I should tell you that views like emotivism are not all that widely accepted in the field of metaethics, and those who think there is such a thing as moral truth, that it is, for example, really true that it is wrong to hurt babies, tend to think that if we can find or articulate a plausible ethical theory about what makes actions right or wrong, then we would no longer need to doubt or worry about the existence of moral truth.

I more than suspect, however, that what might lead some of you to question the idea of looking for moral truth—through philosophical ethics, through divine revelation, or in some other way—is your belief that there is and always has been so much moral controversy, so much moral disagreement, in the world, that it makes no sense to suppose we humans are capable of coming up with a univocally valid understanding of the ethical. That would certainly stop ethics in its tracks, but should we really be so pessimistic? The pessimism depends on the assumption that moral disagreement is practically universal and will inevitably remain so, but on closer reflection we can find reason to question this pessimism.

One consideration that may make you wonder about the possibility of a universal and universally valid (theory of) morality is the sheer variance and even opposition of moral standards that seems prevalent between different societies or cultures. But, to begin with, we shouldn't exaggerate the extent of the differences. In every society or tribe stealing from other members of the society or tribe is considered wrong; similarly with killing, torturing, raping, deceiving people around you. Those common elements come up in one degree or another in the articulated moral codes of different societies—as per the ten commandments. To be sure there are enormous moral variations between societies and even within them. The Eskimo think it is all right to abandon aging parents on the ice floes, and we think parricide is a horrible crime, but this difference marks a common agreed-on element. The Eskimo practice of abandoning parents and leaving them to die is essential to the survival of their society in harsh climatic circumstances. No such issue exists in present-day developed countries, so the understandable horror at the idea of killing one's parents has no dire circumstance to blunt or circumvent it. More generally, such moral disagreements as we seem to find between the Eskimos and ourselves depend on differences in surrounding circumstances, and most moral disagreements are much more disagreements about the facts than about deep moral principles or values. I am not saying that no deep *moral* disagreements exist, but I do want to say that our moral thinking is more held in common than many of us realize before we study ethics. Let me mention one striking example of this.

We believe that it is morally incumbent on us to save lives when and where we can, but we also believe it is wrong to actually take a life, to kill. And we think it is worse to kill than to let someone die, leave someone to die. Consider a fictional super-surgeon who can all on his or her own repair any organ of the human body. One night three automobile accident victims arrive at his (let us say) hospital and are carted into his appropriately enlarged operating room. Each one needs a different organ and, let us assume, none is an appropriate donor to either of the others. However, outside the operating room is a hopeless vagabond who the doctor kindly allows to sleep on the floor every night. The doctor knows, however, that he could harvest the three organs that the accident victims need from this vagabond and use them to save the lives of all three, but he would first have to (painlessly) kill the vagabond, and though he realizes that no one else knows about the vagabond or would know if he, the surgeon, were to kill him, the surgeon hesitates and more than hesitates to kill the one to save the three. He feels strongly that it would be wrong to do so, and does any one, *any one*, of you readers disagree? There are many cases like this where everyone who considers them would come to the same moral conclusion. In that case there is reason to think that there are common human moral standards and that there exists enough common human moral thinking to make it worthwhile for the normative ethicist to ask "what makes some acts right and others wrong?".

This is the main question normative ethicists ask themselves and try to answer, and rationalism vs. sentimentalism, and virtue ethics vs. utilitarianism vs. rule ethics, constitute different theoretical ways in which they have sought to answer that age-old question. That question is common, moreover, to the philosophical traditions of India, China, and the West and to all the other traditions that in some degree rely on them. So we can say it is the main question of *world ethics*, and we shall address it at length in what follows. I shall present what I take to be the most important theories of right and wrong that ethicists have come up with and will not be content with just presenting them. If you want to understand ethics, you need to understand the main arguments that have been given for one and another ethical theory *and the differing philosophical criticisms that can intelligibly be directed to each of them.* That too, then, we be part of the task of the present book.

Let me say, finally, that after the chapters conveying the main philosophical/ethical contents of this book, there is a list of readings containing bibliographical references to the main texts discussed here. I hope this will allow interested readers to further explore the topics and issues we have considered in this quick immersion into ethics.

Chapter 2
Ethical Rationalism

For reasons I have already mentioned I shall begin with a discussion of ethical rationalism, both its strengths and what might turn out to be its weaknesses. I shall begin by telling you what philosophers in both China and the West have thought to be the two main elements of our human moral thinking and what have been, therefore, the main foci of the articulated theoretical attempts to understand the foundations of such thinking, the bases of right and wrong. For some reason neither Plato nor Aristotle recognized the moral centrality of these two elements or factors, but the Roman Stoic philosopher and orator Cicero and the Chinese Confucian thinker Mencius both did, and philosophers up to the present time seem well aware of the centrality of these two factors. We can name them as Cicero did justice and benevolence, but he understood the Latin word for justice in a way that may not be familiar to present-day readers. For Cicero, it is unjust to break a promise or to harm an innocent, and we would be more likely today to characterize such actions simply as wrong. But they are wrong in a very particular way that differs from the wrongness that we understand under the concept of benevolence. For us it is a failure of benevolence and wrong not to benevolently and readily help those who desperately need our help. The wrongness that arises out of the moral duty of benevolence is thus a wrongness of *omission*. But when we break a promise or harm someone, that is a sin or wrongness of *commission*. This is the kind of action Cicero thought of as falling under the notion of justice, and of course the previously mentioned case of the surgeon is of similar ilk. Nowadays, the word "deontology" is the term philosophers use to designate the morality of what we must not actively do, the morality of commissions; but benevolence is still the word used for the morality of what it would be wrong to omit.

Every moral theory that has any chance of being acceptable in ethics needs to address these two main parts of our ethical thinking, and both Western ethical rationalism and the moral sentimentalism that has sprung up in Asia and the West offer us differing and distinctive ways of conceiving and "dealing" with them. We shall be speaking of rationalism in what immediately follows, but it is important to note first that there are at least two main kinds of ethical rationalism, the intuitionist kind and the Kantian.

The intuitionist variety is perhaps best known nowadays via the work of the English ethicists W. D. Ross and H. A. Prichard. On their view we have rational insight into such truths as "it is wrong to break a promise" and are also able to rationally understand the relative moral weights of such truths when they clash in a given circumstance. Sometimes, for example, the duty to keep one's promises is overridden by the truth "we have a moral duty to help others when we readily can," as when a child is drowning right in front of us but saving him will force one to break, say, a promise to meet someone at a given time. On other occasions, though, the harm threatened is negligible enough so that the duty to keep one's promises takes precedence over to moral imperative to be helpful. So rationally intuited moral duties can clash, but when they do, Ross and Prichard hold that our rational moral understanding can tell us which takes precedence and lead us, as rational beings, to act accordingly.

However, this approach is no longer considered viable by academic moral philosophers because it doesn't take into account issues about how much to weigh one's own good and that of one's family and friends against the general benevolent injunction to be helpful to others however they may be related to oneself. Moreover, this sort of approach relies on our intuitions as to the truth of particular moral injunctions but doesn't tell us why they are true. Moral philosophers seek to understand why, for example, it is usually wrong to ignore the needs of others, but all the intuitionists tell us is that, given our rational capacities, we know for certain that it is wrong to do so. (We can know for certain that someone is lying without knowing why they are lying.)

Something like the same problem exists for the most influential of ancient forms of ethical rationalism, Aristotle's virtue ethics. On one interpretation of Aristotle, he is claiming that we intuitively know what it is right or noble or ignoble to do in various circumstances but cannot offer a reason to explain why such judgments apply: they are simply basic and are to be taken on faith of reason. On another familiar interpretation of Aristotle, however, what is right or wrong, noble or ignoble to do in given circumstances depends on whether a given action will tend to serve the long-term happiness of the individual moral agent. This, however, seems more self-centered than anything philosophers today find moral-theoretically acceptable, and in fact nothing like this problem arises for the modern intuitionists Ross and Prichard, so in general the various forms of rational intuitionism are not today seen as philosophically promising. Kantian moral rationalism doesn't have these problems and is perhaps best known for its efforts to show why our common duties are duties. It seeks in very general terms to explain why it is wrong to break promises or ignore the welfare of suffering others; in other words, it seeks to explain what makes right acts right and wrong acts wrong, and given the goals of ethical theory as I have stated them above, this gives Kantian rationalism a presently well-recognized advantage over the intuitionist variety. So let us now talk about Kantian ethics.

Kant was born in Koenigsberg in East Prussia and his whole career was spent at the university there. His most famous philosophy developed later rather than earlier in his life; he started his novel thinking when he was already in his fifties. Kant is probably most famous among philosophers for his account of the nature and limits of human knowledge, but we are most interested here in what he had to say about ethics. No other modern figure has had a comparable influence in that area, and I want to explore in both expository and critical fashion his original ideas as an ethicist. Of course, and as I have already said, Kant was an ethical rationalist, but it was a more ambitious form of ethical rationalism than the world had seen at least since the days of Aristotle. Moreover, Aristotle's ethics make use of vocabulary and concepts that differ from those we now find most important to ethical theory and to the moral life itself. We value conscience and regard guilt as an appropriate reaction to wrongdoing, but Aristotle seems to lack these concepts, and as I mentioned earlier there is an egocentric tendency in his thought that differs widely from what we ethical theorists and the general public think about morality today. On one standard interpretation, the main ethical question for Aristotle was: How can I do well in life, how can I live a happy life; but for modern moral-philosophical thinking the main question we should ask is: What are my moral obligations? Kant tries to answer that question and offers us a very deep picture of what lies behind and explains our moral obligations and duties. This is more apposite to present-day moral thinking than worrying about how one can live well, so as compared with Aristotle (and also Plato and the Stoics) his moral philosophy is taken more seriously in and is more influential on contemporary ethics than anything we have from the ancient Western world. In our next chapter I shall tell you about Kant's more recent influence on the doing of moral philosophy, and then subsequently I will also critically contrast and compare his views with those of moral sentimentalists in India, China, and the recent West. (There were no sentimentalists in ancient Greece and Rome just as there is no tradition of ethical rationalism in China or, I believe, India.)

Kant started with the belief that moral truths hold valid for all rational or intelligent creatures. According to Kant, the wrongness of false promising holds not just for or among us humans but for any possible or imaginable society, and there is something intuitively plausible and even perhaps compelling about this view of the matter. According to Kant, we as rational beings can know that false promising (making a promise in order to obtain something one wants even though one doesn't intend to keep the promise) is wrong without inquiring into issues of anthropology or any other social science; and this then entails that, as we tend to think, the wrongness of false promising holds necessarily in any imaginable circumstance. Kant then tries to explain philosophically *how* such truths are possible and objectively valid in relation to rational beings like ourselves, and that was arguably his main purpose as a moral philosopher. (He also tried to integrate what he was saying about morality with what he had previously said about human knowledge, but we will leave all that to one side.)

Kant famously said that two things in the world filled him with awe: the starry heavens above and the moral law within. For Kant morality consists in something that commands and limits us the way a law does, so to that extent he is neither a virtue ethicist nor a utilitarian. What makes an action right is that it is in accordance with rationally knowable moral laws that command us at all times, so neither what causes us to act nor the consequences of our actions are relevant to their moral status. I have not previously given a name to this third of the three approaches Jorge Garcia distinguished in terms of their temporal assumptions, but (in Kant's honor) we can call it moral law ethics. Sometimes, however, Kant's rationalistic law approach is called deontological, where deontology is the name philosophers give, roughly, to the idea that killing is worse than letting die. Our surgeon example and the reluctance we all feel about saying that it is morally acceptable for him to kill the vagabond in order to harvest his organs and save three lives in the only way that is possible for him illustrate how deeply ordinary moral thinking is committed to deontology. By contrast, the typical utilitarian says that, other things being equal, the surgeon should kill the vagabond because in the circumstances that will have overall better consequences for human happiness than if he refrains from doing so and lets the accident victims die. This shows how deeply utilitarianism disagrees with ordinary moral thinking, and that explains why so many philosophers, including Kant and those mainly influenced by his thinking, try to defend deontology as rationally incumbent on us. But rather than, in intuitionist fashion. just claim that utilitarianism is clearly, intuitively, wrong on this issue, Kant seeks to explain *why* deontology is valid and utilitarianism mistaken and to do so within the larger context of a general explanation of what makes acts right or wrong. Clearly, this is a bold philosophical venture, and we are going to examine its details and consider just how well it holds up under critical scrutiny.

Early in his *Groundwork of the Metaphysics of Morals*, Kant makes a striking statement. He says that nothing in the universe has absolute or unconditional value except a good will. Now this famous passage is not referring to good will in the ordinary sense of the world, as when we speak of "men of good will." That phrase refers to individuals who are benevolent toward others, but Kant isn't talking about benevolence. No, rather, the phrase "good will" refers to pure moral conscientiousness, the desire to do one's moral duty because one knows it is one's duty. Kant says that talents have value only if they serve good purposes: the coolness of a villain in the commission of a crime is a bad, rather than a good, thing. Similarly, he says that happiness or doing well in life is not unconditionally good in the way ancient philosophers like Plato and Aristotle held. No, the happiness of a mass murderer is or would be, from an objective standpoint, a regrettable, a bad thing. By contrast, he says acting out of respect for the moral law is always a good thing.

Now this claim together with what Kant says about the starry heavens and the moral law within shows that Kant wants to defend what I have called a moral law ethics, and that defense goes forward in a very particular way in the *Groundwork*. He argues that it is morally better to act out of a good will, or as we might say conscientiously, than to be motivated by such morally unself-conscious motives as benevolence or compassion. These latter can sometimes go morally astray, as would occur if a judge sentenced a convicted murderer to brief jail time out of compassion for what their family would suffer in their absence and without considering their past or possible future victims. But Kant thinks conscientiousness cannot be corrupted or overdone in this way and so wants to claim that only acting from respect for the moral law can count as morally admirable or good. Here, and as we shall see later at some length, Kant is at odds with the sentimentalist tradition and its central emphasis on motives and moral virtues like compassion. Rationally knowable universally valid morality must, he thinks, be based in pure rationality rather than in something he says is variable and contingent like feeling or emotion.

Having said as much, Kant makes a strong further move. If respect for the law is the sole admirable or virtuous moral motive, then, he argues, the laws that govern normative morality must be *about* lawfulness and its universal morally binding character. This is a controversial further step, but it leads Kant to what is possibly the best-known feature of his moral philosophy, his reliance on what he calls the *Categorical Imperative*. Kant says that if our normative moral laws must be about universal lawfulness itself, then the following must be the basic law governing all morality: Act only on policies or intentions (what Kant calls "maxims") that you could will to be universal laws. He calls this the Categorical Imperative, but it turns out that he thinks this isn't the only way one can express the fundamental basis of moral law and morality. I will say more about that a bit later, but for now the important point is that Kant thinks all of our ordinary moral thinking about what is or is not our duty can be subsumed under the above-stated Categorical Imperative. It is, for example, our duty to give some help to those who need our help because no (rational) person could possibly will that no one ever intentionally help anyone else. One can't will that no one be willing to help one if one ever needs help—and everyone needs help some of the time.

Kant goes on to derive other common or common-sense moral duties from his Categorical Imperative. For example, he argues that false promising couldn't be or be willed as a universal practice or policy because no one would then believe anyone's promises and promising as a tool of communication and social interaction would simply become impossible. Some of Kant's attempts at derivation seem more successful than others, but it should be clear what Kant is trying to do. He is saying that the rational validity of the Categorical Imperative explains the validity of all our ordinary moral duties, and this would mean that he had achieved the main goal of ethics: to explain why certain sorts of acts are morally wrong and others morally all right or permissible.

The observant reader may also have noticed how similar Kant's Categorical Imperative (CI) is to the familiar "Golden Rule." The latter says "do unto others as you would have them do unto you." The CI says in effect: do unto others as you would have everyone do unto everyone. One or another version of the Golden Rule can be found in many cultures (Confucius enunciates a negative version of it); but Kant's CI represents a more abstract and universal form of Golden Rule, and it is no wonder that Kant should have conceived and proposed it as the universal basis of morality.

One well-known problem with the CI as stated above, however, is that it morally rules out too much. It tells us, for example, that it is wrong to be intent on becoming a postal worker (like one's mother) and have no other work interest or aspiration. After all, no one could want everyone to have a similar strong intention or aspiration. This kind of difficulty has led some followers of Kant to emphasize another of Kant's formulations of the CI as the ultimate basis of morality. (Kant himself never recognized this problem with the first statement of the CI.) They prefer the "Formula of Humanity" version of the CI that Kant proposes a little bit later in the *Groundwork*.

Kant attempts to prove that formula in a somewhat complex way. He first points out that ordinary objects are used by us in accordance with ends or goals we have set for ourselves. According to Kant, the objects we seek are ends only in relation to our seeking them. They are just means to the satisfaction of our ends, but we rational humans are *ends intrinsically or in ourselves*. This certainly stretches the notion of an end beyond our usual understanding of it, but assuming that we are intrinsic ends in some intelligible sense, Kant goes on to derive what is called the Formula of Humanity (FH), according to which we should never treat other people (and ourselves) as mere means to our ends but should always at least partly treat them as ends in themselves. How this moral formula or "imperative" follows from the supposed fact that we are ends in ourselves and, earlier on, from the actual fact that we set ends is far from a clear matter. But many philosophers think that the FH is more morally persuasive than the first version of the CI and have relied on it for the derivation of our ordinary moral thinking. This makes some intuitive sense because we do feel most of us that there is something wrong with merely using people. However, when someone pays a taxi driver to take them somewhere, they need not be merely using the person. They may be willing to pay a reasonable fare even if they know they might get away with paying less or cheating the driver altogether. So there is intuitive force behind the FH even if Kant's proof of its validity leaves much to be desired.

This, however, needn't be a very undesirable result for Kant. He could say or one could say on his behalf that even if he cannot prove the FH, there is reason to accept it on the sheer grounds of its intuitive or rational plausibility. In that case, if the FH allows us to derive the duties that are commonly accepted in morality, he can say that this version of the CI can be used to explain why the kinds of actions we usually consider right are right and why those we usually consider wrong are wrong. This also means Kant would be able to explain why we have the moral obligations we have because to say something is obligatory is simply to say it would be wrong not to do it. The main goal of moral philosophy would thereby have been accomplished much to Kant's eternal philosophical/ethical credit.

Now Kant is generally considered a deontologist in the sense stated above; in fact he is thought to be the clearest and most thoroughgoing deontologist ethics has ever known. But I want to show you now that the FH, however valid it may be, doesn't help to support the deontology that we all commonsensically tend to accept, the deontology that tells us that apart from further consequences it would be wrong for the surgeon to kill and harvest the organs of the vagabond in order to save the three accident victims.

Consider the case of the surgeon. If he decides to harvest the organs and perform the multiple relevant operations, does he treat the vagabond as a mere means? Certainly, it might at first seem so, but think about what the utilitarian who rejects deontology might say about the case. They might analogize with situations in which one has to choose between ten people in danger of drowning a mile away from one on the left and thirty people in similar danger at a similar distance to one's right. One owns a big boat that can fit thirty people, but if one saves the thirty the ten will drown. Morality seems to tell us that other things being equal we should save the thirty, but surely this doesn't involve treating or regarding anyone as a mere means. One may regard all the people at risk as having lives one has reason to want to save, lives that are not just means to the enjoyment or purposes of further parties. It's just that thirty valuable lives count morally for more than ten do, and so it is morally incumbent on the boat owner (we most of us think) to save the thirty rather than the ten.

But, some will say, the case of the surgeon is different; it involves a choice between active killing and allowing people to do. Surely, in cutting up the body of the vagabond, the surgeon would be using him for rescue purposes. Yes, that is true, but consider what the utilitarian can say about the case. They can point out that the surgeon may very well think the vagabond's life is in itself valuable, that is, valuable independently of whether it can be taken to serve the needs of others. Like what happens in the boat case, they may also think that three valuable lives morally count for more than one, and it is that fact that may make them claim the surgeon should kill the vagabond. In that case the vagabond is not being viewed as a mere means in the sense of the FH, and so the utilitarian insistence that one should kill the vagabond is just as consistent with the FH as the deontologist's claim that it would be wrong to kill him. The Formula of Humanity thus offers no way to justify deontology, and Kant gives us no other plausible way of doing so, so Kantian ethics gives us no answer to the question why, as we commonly think, we shouldn't kill one innocent person in order to save three. (If it is a matter of saving a million or even a hundred lives, common sense may hold a different opinion.)

Interestingly, many present-day Kantians accept this result, and the philosopher David Cummiskey has even written a widely read book called *Kantian Consequentialism* that is based on the rejection of deontology. But most ethicists reject utilitarianism and the whole idea of basing morality only on good consequences (this is called consequentialism) because it goes against the grain of our deepest and seemingly most universal common/intuitive moral beliefs. That Kantian ethics ends up in the same boat is reason to question its ultimate validity as an account of the moral, but some will say that this point doesn't completely undermine Kantianism because *every theoretical approach to ethics has difficulty justifying deontology.* (We shall see how this bears on moral sentimentalism in a later chapter.)

All this doesn't, however, leave Kantian ethics even temporarily off the hook, because apart from the issue of deontology, Kantian ethics persistently finds itself with problems justifying or thus explaining certain important aspects of ordinary moral thinking. We saw this with the first, the universal willing, version of the CI—remember the issue of being committed to becoming a postal worker. But the FH also has problems justifying and explaining the validity of ordinary morality, though the problems are quite different from those that challenge the universal willing version of the CI.

The FH takes off from Kant's assumption or conclusion that human beings are ends in themselves because of their capacity as rational beings to set goals or ends. The formula tells us how we should treat rational beings like other people and ourselves but puts no restrictions on how we should deal with animals. It places no moral limit on the ways we may treat animals, and this is far from the way all or most of us regard the matter. We think it is morally incumbent on us not to be cruel to animals, but nothing in the FH tells us we shouldn't be since it doesn't include them as "ends in themselves."

In addition, there are moral issues about benevolence toward other human beings that the FH is inadequate to deal with. It tells us we shouldn't treat any person entirely as a means, but if I give a beggar or suffering other a small amount of help when I could easily do more for them, morality, our morality, will criticize us for doing less than we should even though to the extent of our minimal charity or helpfulness we are not treating them as mere means. I mentioned in chapter 1 that there are thought to be two main parts of morality: benevolence and justice. It seems that the FH offers an inadequate account of our moral duties both of benevolence and of justice.

Now utilitarianism and the consequentialism it entails put a great moral emphasis on benevolence or beneficence, on helping others. But in standard versions it says we ought to do the most we can in every situation to advance the welfare or happiness of humanity (or sentient beings generally). That means that if a doctor could always do more good if they never took a summer vacation, it would be wrong of them ever to do so, and common-sense would regard this as too demanding, as unfair to the life of any doctor. So in intuitive common-sense terms, Kantianism demands too little benevolence and utilitarianism too much. Can we find a happy middle ground? Later on, we shall have to see whether moral sentimentalism can do any better.

But we should now move our discussion forward in time. We need to consider ethical thinkers who have subsequently been influenced by Kant and ask ourselves whether their work represents an improvement over the limitations we have found in Kantian ethics. Even if Kant's ethics in itself doesn't ultimately pan out, it brought important ideas into the field of ethics (and more generally), and it has inspired many recent ethicists to try to improve on ideas and views for which Kant laid the groundwork (pun, I guess, intended).

Chapter 3

The Kantian Influence

It is interesting what has happened to Kant's moral philosophy over the more than two centuries after he wrote. In Germany the most important philosophical figure immediately after Kant was G. W. F. Hegel, who is perhaps best known today for his influence on Karl Marx's "dialectical materialism." In the particular area of ethics, Hegel had a rather negative attitude toward Kant's moral philosophy, and what Hegel said about ethics led to the widespread view, both in Germany and in the English-speaking world, that Kant's Categorical Imperative was nothing but an "empty formalism," that in the end all it was good for was for telling us that ethical truths have to have universal implications: that if something is wrong in one circumstance it has to be wrong in any very similar circumstance. Well, this latter claim, which is sometimes called the universalizability of the moral, is certainly not very informative about what counts as morally acceptable or morally wrong. But if you think about it, the versions of the CI we examined in the last chapter go far beyond any such pure formalism. Kant used them to explain in a non-trivial fashion what was right or wrong in particular cases, and the criticisms we earlier made of Kant's use of the CI was not that it is trivial but that it leads to implausible moral results.

For the whole nineteenth century and early twentieth century Kantian ethics was mainly and mistakenly viewed as trivial and as leading us to no interesting substantive conclusions about right and wrong. Then, in the 1950's, a young philosopher named John Rawls started trying to revive Kantian ethics and show its underappreciated merits. At that time, virtue ethics either in Aristotelian or in sentimentalist form was unknown to Western philosophers; for various reasons Aristotle's ethics had died too deep a death in the seventeenth century to be taken seriously in the 1950's; and sentimentalism was largely unthought of as a way of doing or understanding philosophy. The only moral philosophy that, in the English-speaking world, had any important role was utilitarianism, and the influential nineteenth-century utilitarian Henry Sidgwick had like all the others dismissed Kantian ethics as in some sense trivial. But Rawls thought differently and sought to develop an ethics bearing strong Kantian influence that could work as a Kantian reply to all the previous doubts and to utilitarianism as the then dominant theoretical approach to moral philosophy.

But Rawls was more interested in finding a political philosophy than in formulating an account of individual right or wrong action. Utilitarianism tells us that individual actions should produce the best available consequences for human happiness, but it also tells us, analogously, that the laws or institutions of a country are just if and only if they produce the best results that can be produced in the circumstances. Rawls sought to produce and eventually did produce a political philosophy that conceived social justice in terms that largely bear the influence of Kant. (There is some controversy about whether Rawls should simply be called a Kantian.) In a series of articles and then in his highly influential 1971 book *A Theory of Justice*, Rawls explains at length why he thinks utilitarian accounts of social justice are less plausible than his own Kantian-influenced view, which he called "justice as fairness."

Rawls's arguments are highly interesting and can hardly be called trivial. Kant had said that social justice consists entirely in the maximization of individual or civil liberties within any given society, and Rawls borrowed from Kant to a certain extent by claiming that the most important element of social justice in a modern-day society is the maximization of *equal* civil liberties for everyone. Such a view, taken on its own, is an example of what we call libertarianism, but Rawls was not a libertarian but rather a liberal in the present-day sense of the term. Unlike the libertarian, the liberal thinks that a just society must, in addition to securing basic freedoms, institute a safety net to mitigate poverty and the worst effects of social inequality. Rawls takes this last idea in a very specific and novel direction, claiming that social justice requires society and the legal/political system to raise the standard of living of those worst off in society to as high a level as possible. This last idea he labeled the "difference principle" because it entails that differences in social burdens and benefits should always be to the greatest possible benefit of those worst off in society. Rawls included this principle in his theory or conception of justice and to that extent went beyond libertarianism by expressing a substantial and necessary concern for the welfare of members of a given society. But his view also deserves to be called liberalism because he treats the institution and preservation of civil liberties and democratic rights as taking complete precedence over considerations having to do with how well off people are.

This gives you a brief but representative picture of Rawls's theory of justice, but of course we will want to know how Rawls seeks to show its superiority to the utilitarianism that ruled the philosophical roost at the time he was writing. To that end, Rawls employed a kind of social contract theory. Ever since before Plato, some philosophers have sought to conceive a good or just society as one that comes about though an agreement or "social contract" among those who are going to live in the society. But unlike some of the philosophers in that tradition, Rawls didn't think any such contract had ever, historically, actually been agreed upon. Rather, his idea was that social justice can best be conceived as a system of rules that *would* or *could* come to fruition if those who were going to live in a given society had to decide which rules to adopt and commit themselves to under conditions that were morally acceptable or fair for the making of such an agreement. (It should be clear, I hope, that we can see notions like fairness and justice as fundamentally moral notions.) Rawls attempted to describe conditions that he thought were fair for the coming to such a general agreement or contract and then to show that under those conditions for contractual agreement, his two principles would be preferred to utilitarianism (whose basic tenet is that we should maximize overall human welfare or happiness).

How does Rawls seek to accomplish this? Well, to begin with he thinks a fair agreement is much more likely to occur if those who are asked to come to agreement don't know about their own particular talents. The society should be fair to one no matter how talented or untalented one is, so Rawls imposed a "veil of ignorance" on his potential contractors that deprives them of any knowledge that could bias their choice of rules or laws to live by. General knowledge of human psychology and of social science generally doesn't seem to favor anyone in the absence of particular knowledge of their talents or other circumstances, so Rawls treats his contractors as knowing general laws about human nature.

The general requirement of Rawls's contractual situation is that those who commit themselves to an emerging system of social rules do so in entire good faith, and that gives Rawls the basic ingredients of his argument for the superiority of his justice as fairness over utilitarian ideas about justice. Utilitarianism tells us that we have to maximize human happiness even if such maximization involves raising the prospects of the majority of citizens *at the expense of some smaller group of citizens.* One should sometimes help the many even if that means hurting the few. Most of us don't think that would be fair, but Rawls's very clever point is that people won't in general stand for being put at a great disadvantage for the sake of piling great advantages on others. Given their knowledge of human nature, Rawls's contractors would know that they very well might not be willing to accept a very disadvantaged socio-economic position if, under utilitarian rule and given their possible lack of talent, they turned out to be the ones who were being asked to accept a bad lot in life so that many, many others could do much better. So on Rawls's view the contractors cannot in all good faith commit themselves to abiding by utilitarian social policy if such a policy ended up requiring them (with, say, their lack of talents) to be greatly disadvantaged. (Rawls speaks here of the "strains of commitment.") By contrast, Rawls's principles of justice, which raise the level of the worst off as high as possible, don't imply any similar strains of commitment for those who are asked to commit themselves to basic laws or rules of society. They would thus in all good faith choose Rawls's principles of justice over utilitarianism and since the conditions of the choice are presumed to be fair ones for the making of such a choice, Rawls has an argument to show that his theory of justice is superior to utilitarianism.

Now many philosophers have questioned Rawls's argument here. But I myself think that he does a pretty good job of it. The only problem for me is with the principles of justice Rawls argues for. Rawls himself says that if a moral-theoretic argument leads to moral conclusions that we find initially and intuitively implausible, the original argument comes into question. And that is just what I think about Rawls. The argument is quite possibly successful in its own terms, but I am convinced that Rawls's conception of social justice has implications for society that are morally dubious and even, possibly, offensive. However, I am not going to go any further into this until I discuss subsequent work by Rawls's students and admirers that seems to me to have the same morally invidious social implications, something I plan to do a bit later in this chapter.

Rawls had a number of distinguished admirers and students who took his liberalism further: among them, T. M Scanlon, Thomas Nagel, Stephen Darwall, and Ronald Dworkin. (Others of Rawls's students showed more interest in Kant than in Rawls himself.) I want to discuss some of their main contributions to political philosophy and also to the ethics of individuals, and I will begin with Scanlon. His book *What We Owe to Each Other* takes Rawls's views about the moral-political relevance of social contracts and applies them to individual morality. It also deliberately goes beyond Kant in a way that helps us better understand the rationalist understanding of moral motivation.

Kant constantly talked about rationality and held that rational individuals who rationally understood the truth of certain moral principles or laws would automatically be motivated to act in accordance with those laws. But this raises a question, a problem, because a critic might argue that it is one thing to know truth and quite another to be motivated by that knowledge toward *doing something*. What right does Kant have to assume that his moral principles will guide rational individuals in their actions? (This is sometimes framed as the question: how can we know that the rational knowledge of moral truth is *practical*?) I would like now to discuss with you how Kantian-influenced followers of Rawls sought to solve this problem and do so more convincingly than Kant does.

Scanlon relied on a move Thomas Nagel made earlier in his book *The Possibility of Altruism*. Though Nagel himself never puts things this way, that book offers a very clever and original solution to the motivational problems raised by Kant's reliance on the notion of rationality and practical rationality. Rather than talk in the large about rationality, Nagel tells us how to think about *reasons for action*. If I want a coke and know that I can only get one if I put money in a vending machine, then I have reason or a reason to put money in that machine. But of course that reason depends on a prior desire, and Nagel holds that some of our (practical) reasons don't depend on prior (egocentric) desires but exist independently of and antecedently to such desires. Nagel's examples of this are very interesting, but I propose to switch to the use Scanlon makes of this new apparatus to focus on moral reasons for action rather than rationality overall in the way Kant did. According to Scanlon, any normal person can see that they have a reason to help someone who needs help or, to take an amusing historical example, a reason not to step on someone's gouty toes. This reason is moral insofar as it relates to the welfare of others, but here it the interesting new point:

> One cannot believe or recognize that one has a reason to do something without having some motivation toward doing it. (Other

motives might in the end interfere with one's actually doing it.) This is clearly true in the case of the coke machine: even though the person who wants a coke may not think of themselves as having a reason to put money in the machine, they would agree that they do if one raised the issue with them. *But once one agrees, once one knows, that one has (a) reason to do something, one cannot fail to have some motivation toward doing the thing.* So in this case knowledge entails motivation, and the same point holds analogously if one can perceive that one has a reason not to step on someone's gouty toes. So on Scanlon's view as influenced by Nagel's earlier work, moral motivation is automatic in the light of morally relevant knowledge. Kant's problem of getting from moral knowledge to moral motivation seems effectively, then, to be solved. But there is a philosophical cost here too.

How in fact does one know that one has a reason not to step on the toes? Scanlon's answer is that just as we can via our senses perceive objects in space, we can also in another way perceive such things as reasons. We can do this via our capacity for reason. But even though the person who wants a coke may well grant they have reason to put money in the vending machine, they would be puzzled if you told them that they *perceive* their reason to do that. Scanlon holds that reasons have ways of appearing to us that go beyond anything sensory, but one wonders whether this is just a way of trying to save his post-Kantian account of moral motivation. For Scanlon there exist such things as moral reasons though our senses aren't capable of perceiving them; and we are then capable of perceiving and knowing about those reasons in another way. But for the life of me I have never been aware of this kind of thing, and I don't think ordinary folk have been either. On Scanlon's view, furthermore, these existent reasons don't exist in nature around us or even within the mind, so he holds that there exist things that exist outside the natural world but that we have to posit in order to make sense of our moral life and moral thought.

This represents what in effect is a Kantian "transcendental argument." Kant thought nothing was more obvious than that we are bound by certain moral obligations, and he argued that there has to be a world beyond the natural world of space and time for such a thing to make sense. So Kant's anti-naturalism is anchored in what he takes to be the irrefutable fact that we are bound by certain moral obligations. Scanlon doesn't posit a whole non-natural world beyond our own, but he does say, more limitedly, that there exist reasons that aren't part of nature and that such entities have to exist if morality is to have the validity and practical action-guiding influence it is supposed to have. However, all of this might persuade someone to give up on the whole idea of objectively valid morality, or as an alternative one might try to find a way to accept that validity without having to presuppose non-natural entities. I am going to propose just such a way, a sentimentalist way, in a later chapter, but for now we can see that Scanlon's approach only softens the problems that arise out of Kant's ethics rather than eliminating them altogether. More generally, the whole idea of a world or entities that exist outside of nature is hard to intellectually swallow, and to that extent Scanlon's approach is deeply open to critical questioning. We have to try to do better.

In the aforementioned book Scanlon also goes on to offer a contractualist model of individual right action that is highly analogous to the contractualism Rawls proposed for understanding social justice. But I want to delay till a bit later my criticisms of the moral theory Scanlon presents and defends. I shall then go into criticisms not only of Scanlon's views, but also of Nagel's, Dworkin's, Rawls's, even Kant's ideas about the nature both substantively and methodologically of the moral realm. I leave Darwall out of this list because I have different things to say about his views, and I shall address his approach in what immediately follows.

Over the years, Stephen Darwall has defended both Kantian and Rawlsian types of view. He theorizes in fact about a number of different moral topics, but here I want to focus on what he says by way of defending Kant's views about the moral worth of human beings. If you recall, Kant says that human being are ends in themselves, but he also claims that all humans have moral worth. Some people may be more morally admirable than others, but all human beings are, he thinks, equally worthy of our moral respect because of their inherent rational capacities. Darwall runs with these ideas by specifying two kinds of respect: appraisal respect and recognition respect. The former is closely related to Kant's idea that we can have a higher or lower opinion of someone's moral character: we consider some people virtuous and others vicious and there can be degrees of such description. Darwall offers an account of recognition respect that takes on subject matters not immediately relevant to morality, but he then uses this notion to claim, in Kantian manner, that all humans, however vicious, are entitled to this kind of respect because of their equal moral worth. However, as my colleague and friend Berit Brogaard and I agree, this stretches the notion of moral worth, and consequently the concept of respect, beyond any ordinary notion of it. There seems to be no sense in which Hitler was as morally worthy as his victims and *for that reason* deserving of the same respect as those victims. Kant introduced the notion of respect into moral philosophy, and we today think respect is a very important value, an important moral value, but Kant and Darwall's ways of describing and justifying respect don't really hold water, and I hope to show you later that there are other, better ways in which to encapsulate the moral importance of respect.

It is now time for us to consider the way or ways in which Dworkin, Nagel, and Scanlon (DNS) argue for something like Rawls's views about the nature of just societies. As we saw above, Rawls treats equal civil liberties as prior to considerations of human welfare in a just society, and DNS go along with this view and seek to support it in ways that Rawls never engaged with. Civil liberties are named in the American Bill of Rights and include such things as the right to freedom of movement, the right of free speech, the right of free assembly, and the right to worship freely as one chooses (religious freedom). Focusing mainly on free speech and freedom of assembly, DNS seek to show that it takes precedence over considerations of welfare in situations that Rawls himself never explicitly spoke of, and an argument almost exactly parallel to the one they make can be used to argue for the priority of freedom of individual movement over welfare.

The case or situation DNS mainly focus on concerns the town of Skokie, Illinois, where in the 1970's neo-Nazis requested permission to march through the streets and assemble a crowd to hear speeches vilifying the races and religions the Nazis have always had it in for. There were a large number of Jewish Holocaust survivors living in that town, and it is supposed that that was the main reason why the neo-Nazis asked for permission to march and speechify there rather than in some other town or venue. The march, in the end, never took place, but followers of Rawls like DNS argued that the march should have been allowed. (There was never, in fact, a court decision *not* to allow it.) DNS followed Kant and to a lesser extent Rawls in attempting to justify the legal and moral permissibility of the march and speech-giving by reference to the value of autonomy. According to DNS freedom of speech, assembly, and the like are manifestations of the value we place on autonomy, on rights of autonomy. Here autonomy is not understood as a metaphysical reality as Kant held. Kant thought our autonomy is a matter of our ability and freedom to act independently of all natural inclinations and desires, but for DNS autonomy comes down partially to earth as, less metaphysically, the right to express ourselves as moral individuals through our own free and unimpeded choices as to what to say, how to worship, where to meet, etc.

DNS take it that these autonomy rights and most especially the right to freedom of speech and the right of free assembly take precedence over other factors that might make the neo-Nazi march and speechifying seem morally unpalatable to many of us. Such a march and such making of speeches in the immediate vicinity of where one lives will very likely give deep offense to those who live there, but DNS argue that autonomy rights take or should take moral/legal precedence over any offense the surrounding population might feel at what was going on. But here is the most interesting point. DNS never mention the possibility, indeed the likelihood, that the neo-Nazi event would have a deeper impact on the Holocaust survivors. They would be likely to be more than just offended by or unhappy with the neo-Nazi happenings; those happenings would be quite likely to *retraumatize* many of the Holocaust survivors. This means more than offended or hurt feelings, it means that there very possibly would be a lot of psychological damage or harm done to the survivors if the march and speechifying were allowed to go forward. But this fact or factor is (surprisingly enough because two of them are Jewish) totally ignored by DNS.

Moreover, when the moral philosopher Susan Brison went and pointed this out to them, they didn't change their political/legal evaluation of the issue about Skokie. They still maintained that the march should have been allowed on grounds of human rights of autonomy. This clearly involves treating autonomy-based civil liberties as morally taking precedence over (even) considerations of harm or damage or, more generally, welfare, and that is precisely what Rawls's prioritized principles tell us is socially just. If we disagree with or have doubts about what DNS and, implicitly, Rawls tell us about the Skokie case, then we are calling into question what Rawls and the others have to say about the priority of autonomy over welfare, but we need to realize that not everyone wants to deny what they are saying specifically about Skokie. What more forcefully leads some of us to go against the DNS view of Skokie is what their arguments and Rawls's prioritizing of his principles of justice implies about another prominent case in which the weakness of the DNS-Rawls position seems more obvious and apparent.

In the past and in many jurisdictions even today, judges or other magistrates are reluctant (and the law doesn't readily allow them) to immediately issue restraining orders against husbands or boyfriends who their wives or girlfriends say have threatened them (or their children) with violence or have already done violent things to them (or the children). Often further legal/judicial process is or has been required (the husband is given the opportunity to defend himself in court), and this has often meant that women (and/or their children) are (further) injured or even killed before the further process has taken its course. But why has there been so much reluctance to issue the restraining orders (orders of protection) or even have the women protected through additional police patrols, etc.? In large part it is out of a sense of the importance of autonomy rights of freedom of movement. But this means that until very recently the legal/judicial emphasis has mainly been on autonomy rights/civil liberties rather than on the welfare (rights) of women and/or their children, and I think most of us nowadays—and not just feminists and women— would say that the law has erred in placing so much emphasis on autonomy rights and so relatively little on dangers to women and children.

If that is correct, then Rawls has erred in placing civil liberties prior to any considerations of welfare in his theory of social justice, and this also gives us (further) reason to doubt what DNS say about the Skokie case. Their analysis and conclusions depend on the general assumption that autonomy takes precedence over welfare or well-being in the political/legal sphere, an assumption that the example of the restraining orders pretty effectively undercuts.

But what if, you may ask, a given wife is lying about her husband's having abused or threatened her? Won't it then be unfair to the husband if the restraining order is issued on her say-so? In that particular instance an injustice will, I agree, have been done, but the issue is one of administrative or judicial *policy*, and if the lying wife has no previous record of lying to or misleading officials, then the just policy will dictate taking her at her word and issuing a temporary restraining order that will hold valid till the husband has a chance to be heard in court. This much seems morally plausible and even, at this point, obvious, and to that extent, again, it undermines Rawls's insistence on the priority of liberty and what DNS tell us about the Skokie case. We need a better account of what is morally at stake in the Skokie case and in cases where wives or girlfriends are threatened by their husbands or boyfriends, and later in this book I hope to show you that moral sentimentalism has the resources to provide such an account. For the moment, though, we need to say more about the character of sentimentalism and about its history both East and West.

Chapter 4
The Sentimentalist Traditions

The title of this chapter speaks in the plural. Moral sentimentalism has come in many varieties but has also been promulgated and defended in more than one of the world's philosophical traditions. Ethical rationalism, as I have already mentioned, has been exclusively confined to the West: to ancient Greece and Rome and to modern Western philosophy, whose main roots go back to Greece and Rome. So although, as we have seen, there are varieties of ethical rationalism—intuitionistic rationalism contrasts with the Kantian—the fact that sentimentalism is to be found both in the West and in the East makes me feel comfortable speaking in the plural about sentimentalist traditions. Having said as much, we should perhaps go even further. I believe Chinese sentimentalism and Chinese philosophy more generally have much to offer any form of Western sentimentalism that seeks to make good headway in present-day philosophical/ethical circumstances. But Indian philosophy as developed in its most world-famous form, Buddhism, also counts as a form of sentimentalism, so in fact all three of the world's endogenous philosophical traditions have developed forms of moral sentimentalism. Again, that is some reason to speak in the plural.

The Indian philosophical tradition is somewhat older that the Western and the Chinese, and it contains a lot of very impressive argumentation and theorizing. However, because Indian culture tends to be pessimistic about the value of ordinary human life—one finds this not only in Buddhism but in Indian philosophy more generally—most Indian philosophy places little emphasis on the ethical. Buddhism, however, does take up ethical issues in a very serious way, and I would like to begin the present chapter by speaking about the roots and tenets of Buddhism. I will be brief about this because in covering the main possibilities of normative ethical theory here in this book, it is important for us to see whether sentimentalism can be developed in such a way that it represents a serious alternative to rationalism. And I confess to finding Chinese thought and Chinese sentimentalism more relevant than Buddhism to that task.

Buddhism originated from the life and thought of Gautama the Buddha. It has been perhaps more influential in the Far East than in India itself, and of course it has had many followers in the West. The Dalai Lama was once asked to summarize Buddhism in a single word, and the word he chose was: kindness. That is certainly a moral concept, a moral virtue, but it should be said that the Dalai Lama was choosing a more familiar term for what in Buddhism is more formally expressed via the term "compassion." But why is compassion so central to Buddhism? It is central because Buddhism sees human life as full of suffering. Like certain counterparts in the Greek West, Buddhism regards desire itself as a painful lack seeking to end itself, and since all of ordinary life involves desires, Buddhism comes out with a negative evaluation of human life on the whole.

But where does compassion then come in? Well, Buddhism thinks it is best to escape from all the suffering by transcending desire and desirousness in favor of a state familiarly called nirvana. It tells us we should have compassion for all the suffering and attempt to relieve it by leading people away from their desire-filled lives toward nirvana. Now Buddhism also has a metaphysics: it seeks to show that the reality we think we know around us is an illusion. We think we are surrounded by other people and things and we think we have an identity of our own as different from that of other people, but Buddhism argues against all of this. I am not going to rehearse the arguments here. In modern-day philosophical terms they are pretty weak, and in any event this is not a book about metaphysics. I hope and believe we can just assume that there are different things in the world and that we as individuals are and can be different from one another.

Buddhism also assumes that desire is necessarily unpleasant, and this too is something one can call into question. The Gestalt psychologists have done just that, but, again, I don't want to go into their arguments here. Suffice it to say that on whatever grounds compassion is very definitely a moral virtue and even a moral imperative. But surely this cannot be the whole story of ethics. Is it compassion that leads us to refrain from killing one person to save three; is it compassion that makes us think we should keep our promises? No, there is much more to ethics than compassion, so although Buddhist ethics is clearly a form of sentimentalism, we need to go beyond it if we are to have a full enough, complex enough ethics to deal with the complexities and richness of human life. And it really doesn't make sense for us to think, as with Buddhism, that human life is not worth living: in which case we should look for ethical thinking that can help us lead an ordinary life in a morally decent fashion. Let me turn now to another sentimentalism of the East, one that does see complexity, value, and challenge in ordinary human life.

You have all heard of Confucius. He was a kind of mixture between a philosopher and a sage, and of course mainstream Chinese culture and tradition has been called Confucianism in his honor. If you read his *Analects*, you will, I hope, be struck by his wisdom, but Confucius was not a sentimentalist and neither was he any kind of rationalist. He didn't really do ethics in the requisite formal fashion. However, a follower of his who wrote about a century later was very much a sentimentalist. That follower was Mencius (in pinyin Chinese Mengzi), and the book containing his views is called the *Mencius*.

Mencius was in the fullest sense a sentimentalist, and much of what he said anticipates the moral sentimentalism that sprung up in the West during the eighteenth and nineteenth centuries C. E., the moral sentimentalism of (the third earl of) Shaftesbury, Francis Hutcheson, David Hume, Adam Smith, and James Martineau. It also anticipates the more recent development of sentimentalism known as care ethics. So let us say something about Mencius's views.

Mencius thought there were four sentimental, that is, emotional, constituents of morality. Speaking roughly, they were benevolence, justice, deference, and wise moral judgment. We don't think of justice or moral judgment as feelings, and the notion of deference isn't part of modern-day Western concepts of morality. But leaving deference aside if I may, it is important to recognize that Mencius thought both justice and moral judgment had a basis in feeling. Two thousand years later, the philosopher David Hume came to the same conclusion, and I hope to show you in what follows that the idea of anchoring such notions and such realities in feeling is more plausible than might initially appear.

Mencius is a bit vague about justice, but he assumed and we can assume that it involves some aspect of morality that is not included in benevolence. To that extent Mencius's justice should remind us of the deontological view that killing one to save three is morally unacceptable. Benevolence can be regarded as preferring three lives to one, but something, for example, about the situation of the surgeon tells us it would be wrong for him to kill the vagabond in order to save the three accident victims. Mencius doesn't have anything this specific in mind—at least he doesn't say that he does—when he differentiates justice (sometimes his term for it is translated as "righteousness") from benevolence, but he treats benevolence as the most important of the elements of morality even if justice and wise moral judgment are seen as somewhat independent of it.

On Mencius's view we cannot bear to see the suffering of others and our benevolence is responsive to suffering or potential suffering when we recognize it. But in my estimation Mencius doesn't quite have the notion of empathy in this connection. He never speaks of feeling another person's pain or, as Hume would do later, of one person's suffering infusing itself into the mind of an observer. Mencius's sentimentalist ethics remains in a more inchoate or philosophically underdeveloped form than was later attempted by Hume and subsequent others, but my main point to you readers is that he really did have an overall sentimentalist moral philosophy millennia before this emerged, along lines more similar than anything we can find in Buddhism, in eighteenth-century British moral sentimentalism. But let us now proceed to describe the latter somewhat more fully.

The first sentimentalist was Shaftesbury, who, interestingly enough, had been tutored as a young man by John Locke. Locke's ideas influenced American political thought, but he also assumed an atomistic view of human beings that saw each person as originally having interests and needs independently of every other person. Shaftesbury came to reject his teacher's view, though he waited till Locke had died before publishing his dissenting ideas. Shaftesbury argued that far from being isolated atoms, we humans are bound to one another by natural ties of sympathetic feeling. Our nature is then to live in *connection* with others rather than in a basic isolation from them that can be "cured" only by some kind of deliberate social contract. Almost three hundred years later Carol Gilligan inaugurated a form of moral sentimentalism that she designated "care ethics" and that takes off philosophically from the deep fact and imperative of human connection— though apparently Shaftesbury wasn't any kind of influence on Gilligan's thinking. We shall talk below about care ethics, but for the moment let us focus on eighteenth-century sentimentalism.

After Shaftesbury came Francis Hutcheson and, much more influentially, his mentee David Hume. Hume was the first person to talk about what we now call empathy. (He didn't have the word and used "sympathy" to refer sometimes to empathy and sometimes, of course, to sympathy—we will distinguish these later.) Hume based his main moral philosophy on the role of empathy in underwriting our benevolent actions. But he also noticed the difference between considerations of welfare and considerations of justice and by his own admission struggled to give both a sentimentalist basis. Then further, he offered an account of moral judgment that was also based on the idea or reality of empathy. An observer who sees one friend help another will have empathy with the empathy the helping friend has for his needy friend, and this kind of second-order empathy with empathy constitutes for Hume the basis for moral judgment. Thus, like Mencius but in seeming total ignorance of his historical example, Hume thinks both human virtue and human thinking about virtue can be accounted for in basically sentimentalist terms. However, by his own admission Hume got into intellectual trouble when he sought to understand justice and fidelity to promises in sentimentalist terms deriving from empathy, and his problems here in effect opened the door to Kant's view that feeling cannot be the basis of morality. Hume's sentimentalism takes us only so far, and we will want to later consider whether a fuller more consistent moral sentimentalism can now be developed and hold its own against ethical rationalism. (At this point I shall leave Adam Smith to one side because despite his greatness as an economist, his moral views are less influential than Hume's have been.)

The final form of moral sentimentalism I would like to describe for you emerged late in the twentieth century and is called care ethics. As I have indicated, care ethics was inaugurated by Carol Gilligan, and I shall focus here more on this form of sentimentalism than on the historical forms discussed above because I believe it is more philosophically promising than the others. But Gilligan hasn't been the only prominent care ethicist. Soon after her book *In a Different Voice* was published, Nel Noddings picked up the thread and offered a (somewhat sketchy) account of the ideas and implications of a normative care ethics. Subsequent care ethicists have taken matters further, and I count myself among those subsequent thinkers. So let me tell you how the most developed form or forms of care ethics would want to deal with normative issues at the same level of specification and generality as we find in Kant or any of his followers.

Gilligan, Noddings, and subsequent care ethicists have a view of ideal or standard moral motivation that differs sharply from what the Kantians say about it. For Kantians, emotion or feeling-based motivation doesn't enter into morally virtuous action; one should help others out of a sense that it is one's moral duty to do so rather than from sheer unself-conscious benevolence or compassion. The care ethicists, by contrast, hold that the most ideal helping moral actions are directed compassionately or benevolently toward the welfare of others and are not mediated by moral principles or rules telling one that one has an obligation to be helpful. The emphasis (as with Shaftesbury) is on direct connection, and moral rules tend to separate us rather than connect us with people who need our help.

However, care ethicists have had difficulty dealing with deontology, though the difficulties are different from those we unearthed in relation to Kantian ethics. There has also been an issue concerning whether an ethics that emphasizes caring can deal with the very general political and legal issues that any theory of social justice needs to account for. In what follows, I shall describe for you how an ethics of care might deal with these issues or difficulties and might ultimately lay claim to intellectual advantages over ethical rationalism.

For care ethics, the prime example of moral goodness is benevolent action toward another person, action based on empathy with that other person (e. g., one's own child or a distressed stranger). Empathy can very roughly be distinguished from sympathy because in emotional empathy we feel the other person's pain (distress) whereas sympathy is understood to mean the different emotional state of wanting to see someone helped. In sympathy we feel *for* the other rather than feeling *what* the other feels. Care ethicists like Noddings see caring/compassionate actions as based on what we can call empathy but have a difficult time defending deontology on such a basis. So I would like us to consider together whether any form of caring sentimentalism can deal with deontology and do so more plausibly and consistently than Kant and the Kantians are capable of doing.

This might at first seem an impossible task. In the case of the surgeon, benevolent feeling seems to tell us it is all right or even imperative for him to kill the one in order to save the three. If it is wrong for him to do so, it would seem that *something other than feeling* must dictate that conclusion, and surely, we think, that other factor has to be something that stands up to and counters feeling, something reason and rationality are naturally thought to do. If rationalism has a hard time explaining the validity of deontology, then surely, it will be thought, sentimentalism will or would have an even harder time of it. Better, then, to try to revise rationalism than to work within sentimentalism if one wants to give a philosophical defense of deontology.

All of this seems obvious, but I hope to show you that it is mistaken. The above reasoning underestimates the resources of sentimentalism and in particular (surprisingly enough) the role that empathy can play in the justification of deontology. It is time for me to make good on these bold claims.

Empathy is *partial*: rather than respond equally to the woes of any other person, it responds more strongly, is felt more deeply, when it is the suffering of someone one knows and loves rather than that of a stranger or mere acquaintance. Empathy is also *perspectival*: clear and present danger empathically moves us more than equally certain future danger, and perceived near danger to others moves us more than merely known-about danger to distant people. A complete sentimentalist care ethics will need to offer a general criterion of right vs. wrong action just as Kantian ethics attempted to do. We saw that Kant's two versions of the CI, each of which is intended as offering a general criterion of right vs. wrong action, are quite problematic, and the question is: can care-ethical sentimentalism do any better?

I want to propose that an action is morally wrong if and only if it shows its agent as lacking in empathic concern for others. The focus is, of course, the emotions or feelings of given agents, but of course an action like getting dressed in the morning can be morally all right according to the above criterion because, of course, it doesn't show its agent as lacking in empathy or because, equivalently, it doesn't reflect or exhibit any lack of empathy on the part of the agent. Nor does one have to show maximum possible empathy in order for one's actions to count as morally acceptable in accordance with our criterion. Only very empathic caring people would offer to give one of their kidneys to a stranger, and an unwillingness to do that doesn't show a person to be *lacking* in empathy but only at most to be less (wonderfully) empathic than a few highly empathic people are. But if one refuses to go into the water to save a drowning child because it will get one's clothes wet, one's non-action does show one as lacking in empathy, and we could go on to describe a number of relevant further examples. However, I would like now to home in on some specific cases of empathy that not only illustrate its partiality and perspective-taking but also lead us toward an understanding and moral justification of deontology.

As we mentioned above and as Hume was well aware, empathy is more sensitive to, more aroused by, suffering or danger we directly perceive than by suffering or danger we merely know *of*. But I also mentioned that it is more strongly elicited by clear and present danger than by danger that is equally certain or probable in the future. If miners are trapped underground, we feel more empathy for their plight than for future miners who we know will encounter similar danger(s). If someone suggests that we should take any money that has been raised to rescue the currently trapped minors and use it instead to install safety devices that will almost certainly save a greater number of miners' lives in the future, we will find that idea morally distasteful and insensitive. (The Reagan solicitor general Charles Fried once actually made such a suggestion.)

Well, there is another way in which empathy is differentially sensitive and reactive to possible or probable dangers or suffering. We are much more empathically sensitive to danger or disaster that we know we might cause than to danger or disaster that we merely know will occur if we don't act. The death of someone we might decide to *kill* seems much more immediate to us than the death of someone we might just *allow to die*. We empathically, emotionally *flinch* from killing in a way we don't flinch (from the idea of) our not saving someone's life. So the contrast between doing and allowing, between commission and omission, is anchored in our empathic reactions, and if empathy gives the measure of right and wrong, then it is as wrong for the surgeon to kill the vagabond as it would be for a passer-by to refuse to save a child drowning right in front of him in order to save three other children in a different place whose danger from drowning he only knows about through what others have told him. We would say in either case that the person had shown themselves to be lacking in (normal human) empathy, and on the present empathy-based sentimentalist account of normative morality, that would indicate that a surgeon who killed a vagabond and a person who abandoned a near, visible, and audible drowning child would be acting wrongly.

Consider, though, that what we have said doesn't tell us *why* empathy is so important to morality, *why* the sentimentalist and care-ethical criterion of wrong (and therefore right) action offered above is valid for (our) morality. However, we might be excused from providing such a further reason or justification on the grounds that Kantian ethics too doesn't successfully tell us why one or another version of the CI is valid. Kant tried to provide such a justification, but we have seen that what he said about it is somewhat tenuous. Still, Kant would have provided us with a good account of why certain acts are right and others wrong if morality, our common morality, could be derived from the CI in the way Kant believed it could be. We have indicated strong doubts about this issue too, but these distinctions show us that a sentimentalist care ethics would have proved its mettle if its basic criterion can help us explain why certain acts are right and others wrong all across the board. So far we have mentioned some salient and important moral cases where the sentimentalist criterion seems capable of doing that, and I know of no examples where that criterion fails to give us a proper account of right or wrong.

Still, there is a problem, a deep problem with sentimentalism that rationalists have very persistently called to our general philosophical attention. I intend to discuss that problem in our next chapter, where I shall also consider other important issues that divide Kantian ethical rationalism from sentimentalism as exemplified in its most recent incarnation, care ethics. So far, too, I haven't specifically mentioned the virtue-ethical character of the kind of sentimentalist care ethics I embodied in the earlier criterion of right and wrong. That criterion tells us that acts count as wrong if they reflect or show bad agential motivation, and this emphasis on what comes before and motivates human actions clearly qualifies the kind of care ethics I am defending as a form of virtue ethics. (Other, older forms of care ethics aren't stated in virtue-ethical terms.) The question now is whether care-ethical virtue-ethical empathy-emphasizing sentimentalism is as plausible as Kantian ethics. Kantian ethics has flaws we have pointed out in profusion, but if sentimentalism has even bigger problems, then there is more reason to work on and further develop rationalism than to jump over to the project of further developing care ethics.

Chapter 5

Rationalism vs. Sentimentalism

At the end of the last chapter I referred to a problem with sentimentalism that seems to set it at a major disadvantage vis-à-vis ethical rationalism. That problem is the problem of objective validity. Kantian ethics and ethics influenced by Kant treats moral claims as having (the plausible ones) objective validity. They are unequivocally true and, more than that, rationalists suppose that that validity is not merely an artifact of human nature. As Kant claims (and I nodded approvingly) the wrongness of torturing or harming others and of making false promises—promises one has no intention of keeping that one makes in order to gain something good for oneself—seems to hold necessarily, that is, for all possible rational or intelligent beings. (We are not talking about tigers.) But moral sentimentalism has a history of denying such a thing, and to that extent it goes against our strong pre-theoretical opinion that it is *simply true* that the above acts are wrong. Nor, in pre-theoretical terms, does anyone suppose that these things wouldn't have been true if humans had been very different. If sentimentalism is confined to denying the objectivity or truth of all moral judgments or rules, then it is at an immense disadvantage *theoretically* in relation to rationalism because good theories have to square with facts and it seems just to be a fact that certain actions are inherently wrong and criticizable as such. (I am certainly not denying, however, that there can be circumstances when it is morally all right to harm another—say in self-defense.)

If we look back at the history of sentimentalism, we see no intellectual commitment to the objective validity of moral norms. To be sure, Mencius and all other Chinese philosophers never worried or even thought about the issue of moral objectivity, but where that issue arises for sentimentalists, they have invariably avoided claiming that ordinary thinking is right about these matters. Hume notoriously but in a theoretically rich manner speculated about the meaning of moral utterances and judgments. But his most considered view in the *Treatise of Human Nature* was that morality is a humanly necessary or important *illusion*. We have moral feelings of approval and disapproval, but according to Hume's "projectivism" every time we make a moral claim we are confusing our own feelings with something objectively outside of us: we mistakenly project our approval or disapproval into the actions we approve or disapprove of and think of rightness or wrongness as something objectively characterizing those actions when it is no such thing.

However, although this may not be his final view of the matter, Hume also worked on and developed a theory that gives moral judgments a certain amount or degree of objective validity. At times he seems favorable to what we now call "ideal observer" accounts of moral judgment, according to which, when we say something is wrong, we are saying that there is a general tendency in human nature to disapprove of that sort of thing, that all fully informed calm human beings would feel disapproval at the thought of someone doing it. This takes the meaning of moral utterances beyond individual moral feelings and makes it a function of human nature generally, but of course this is involves subscribing to a lesser degree of objectivity than Kant so forcefully attributed to our basic moral thinking. As I said earlier, I tend to agree with Kant on this the way rationalists do and in a way that can be attributed to entrenched pre-theoretical moral thinking. If sentimentalism cannot account for a morality that is fully objective, then despite the problems that exist with rationalism and any relative merits we may find in sentimentalist approaches, rationalism is probably the best place to invest our future philosophical efforts. But I think the situation isn't so dire as that for sentimentalism, and in 2010 I published a book called *Moral Sentimentalism* in which I sought to show that, despite all the previous history of denying full moral objectivity, sentimentalists can defend such objectivity on as strong a philosophical basis as anything to be found in Kantian ethics or ethical rationalism more generally. I am going now to show you what I mean.

The care-ethical sentimentalist assumes that empathic concern for others is morally virtuous. But sentimentalism can also invoke empathy at a metaethical or semantic level. Hume thought that empathy was not only essential to moral virtue, not only normatively important, but was also essential to the making of moral claims or judgments, and though he thought such claims lack any objective validity, it is possible to give an account of objective or valid moral thinking making use of the notion of empathy and of a technique developed by the philosopher of language Saul Kripke called "reference fixing."

Hume based his account of the meaning of moral claims on a very special notion of approval. In ordinary usage, moral approval is a matter of *thinking* something is right, not wrong. But Hume understood "approval" in a purely sentimental way, and I propose to do that here. In a nutshell approval can be seen as a kind of empathy with empathy. When a friend helps a friend in need, they typically do so out of warm empathic concern for the friend, but an observer noticing such action and understanding its significance may be warmed by that display of warmth, and this is what I for short called empathy with empathy. We can call it moral approval (in a sentimental or emotional sense). Hume basically saw this point but he never made a parallel point about disapproval. However, one can. One can be said to morally disapprove of someone's, say, neglect of or cruelty toward a friend when one empathically registers the coldness, the cold-heartedness, that that false friend is displaying toward his supposed friend. The chill constitutes a kind of repulsion at what is being done and to that extent represents a kind of emotional disapproval; and something analogous can obviously be said about being warmed by an agent's warm-heartedness toward their friend.

From here we can get to an account of the meaning of moral claims and judgments that allows them to be as fully objective as anything accepted by ethical rationalism. To do that we need to make adjusted use of Saul Kripke's concept of reference-fixing. Kripke doesn't talk about moral predicates and moral issues, but there is a long sentimentalist tradition of analogizing between color terms and moral terms, and Kripke uses the notion of reference-fixing to help us understand how we use color terms like "red."

Kripke argues that we fix the reference of an ordinary term like "red" and do so for all possible circumstances via some description like "whatever it is in objects that typically causes red experiences in us." If it turns out that a certain reflectance property out there in objects is what tends to cause perceiving "redly," then that external property is what (objective) redness is. And it is or would be that property, even if human beings eventually became color-blind or experienced red objects very differently. So on Kripke's view (which most philosophers accept) objective redness is not relative to human experiential dispositions but, in the form of a reflectance property, is fully out there in objects.

It turns out that the concept of moral goodness, or our term "morally good," works in a somewhat analogous way. We can say that the reference of "morally good" is fixed by the phrase "whatever it is in agents or their actions that causes (sentimental) moral approval in observers." Well, given what we have said such approval is, namely, being empathically warmed by empathic agential warmth, it is clear and it follows necessarily that it is only warm empathic caringness in acts or agents that counts as moral goodness in those acts or agents. Now the argument here is entirely a priori: it makes no specific empirical/scientific assumptions (e. g., about what reflectance property in objects causes us to experience redly). It also makes no assumptions about (the goodness of) human nature. It only says that if there is to be such a thing as moral goodness, it must be a trait or entity that causes empathy with empathy. So this account of how we understand and employ the notion of moral goodness allows such a thing to be an objective matter. (That something exists in a person can be an objective fact.) The reference of other moral terms can be analogously fixed, and so sentimentalism can achieve a parity with rationalism regarding the objective validity of moral claims.

Thus sentimentalism cannot be undermined by pointing out that it doesn't allow for moral truth—quite the contrary. This consequently leaves rationalism without what seems to be its strongest argument against sentimentalism, but now I propose to consider what sentimentalism has to say about political philosophy and social justice in particular. The contrast with Kantian-influenced views of justice like that of Rawls will be instructive and may just lead us to conclude that care ethics has some theoretical advantages over ethical rationalism in the area of law and politics.

Carol Gilligan contrasted her ethics of care with an "ethics of justice," and in its early years care ethics avoided issues about social or international justice and focused solely on caring individual actions and caring personal relationships. It was eventually recognized, however, that thus limited, care ethics would never be able to hold its own against ethical theories that could deal both with individual morality and the social. That led some care ethicists to argue that rather than reject the notion of justice altogether and/or turn away from valid issues of social justice, care ethics ought to develop *its own understanding of social justice*. This mainly meant understanding social justice in sentimentalist terms *analogous* to those that were supposed to govern or cover individual actions. It meant, for example, thinking of laws and political/ legal institutions as just if they show those who promulgate or maintain them as caring about the members of society or at least not as lacking in such caring concern for the other members of society. Laws can show or express empathic concern if passing or maintaining them reflects empathy for those affected on the part of those who pass or maintain them, and it could then be argued, for example, that social welfare programs can be considered just in these terms because, e. g., a refusal on the part of a legislature or judiciary to create or allow such programs arguably shows them as lacking in empathic concern for the very poor. (The psychology literature on empathy tells us that empathy for groups of people is just as possible as empathy for individuals.) Proceeding in such a sentimentalist vein, the care ethicist can equate the just society with one whose laws and institutions reflect relevant empathic concern. But of course this is a far cry from traditional ways of conceiving social justice. How can justice possibly turn out to be so very different from the way it has always been theorized?

The care ethicist's best answer to such skepticism will be if they can point out implications of traditional thinking about justice that don't square with our basic understanding of morality and then show that care ethics gets these matters right. And we already have the beginnings of such an argument in what was said about autonomy rights in chapter 3. I there argued that in the Skokie case and, more clearly, in the case of threatened spousal abuse, the rationalist emphasis on autonomy leads one to morally implausible and even unacceptable conclusions. The wife or girlfriend should be immediately granted a protection order against the male in the threatened violence case (I won't bring in LGTBQ variations), and the Kantian thinking of Rawls and of DNS doesn't allow for this political/legal disposition of the issue. Can the justice thinking of the care-ethical sentimentalist do any better?

It can be said for the traditional Kantian thinking that it can be very frustrating for a husband (or boyfriend) to have their freedom of movement restricted, and that is why overall and in general there is no law against going wherever one wants (subject to restrictions arising from property ownership). But the care ethicist will then be able to point out that any frustration on the part of the husband due to restrictions on his movements is far less significant than the likelihood or even the definite possibility that he will harm the wife or his children. Though empathy may be sensitive to frustration and seek in general to avoid frustrating people, it is far more aroused by threats of harm, and that means that an ethics of care based on the criterion offered earlier can and will say that it is wrong to allow the threatening husband the freedom to harm if that is the only way to avoid frustrating him as to freedom of movement. The old rules that mandated a hearing with the husband before the imposition of restraining orders show a certain lack of empathy for women on the part of the older jurisprudence. Today most jurisdictions and laws do much or somewhat better, so care ethics gets matters right in cases where autonomy and safety/welfare clash, and, therefore, despite its unfamiliarity and initial oddness, it makes sense to conceive justice in sentimentalist terms, more sense than a Kantian reliance on and prioritizing of autonomy (rights) can do. Unless the Kantian can find problems with sentimentalist justice on other grounds, we have at least some reason to take it every bit as seriously as we ethicists have always taken Kantian views.

Moreover, just as care ethics is able to substitute its own distinctive conception of social justice and defend it against Kantian disagreement, it clearly can offer its own view of autonomy and autonomy rights, one that places these in a less central position in social morality than Kantianism does. But I won't go into the details. Rather, I would like to speak now about another concept that is important to Kantian thought, the concept of respect. Utilitarianism has no central place for this concept and neither does Aristotelian or neo-Aristotelian virtue ethics, but this for most ethical theorists constitutes a disadvantage and strike against those views. We nowadays are convinced that respect has an important place/role in the morality of individuals and whole societies, and it is to the great credit of Kant that he was the first to introduce this notion into moral philosophy. However, as we saw in chapter 3, Kant—and following him Darwall—introduced the notion of respect via the dubious assumption that all human beings are of equal moral worth—the moral worth of Hitler being the same as that of his victims. We need to find a more plausible way to introduce or understand the respect that we owe to one another, and sentimentalism has in fact of way of dealing with this issue.

Let me start by giving you an illustrative example where people show a *lack of respect*. Imagine that you are a sixteen-year-old girl living at the turn of the twentieth century. You tell your parents you hope to be a doctor when you are older and are met with the rejoinder: you can't possibly want that, dear; you'd be much happier as a nurse or stay-at-home mother. This response brushes aside the daughter's (let us assume) very real aspiration and denies it even exists. This is clearly disrespectful on the part of the parents, and it also shows an unwillingness or inability on their part to see things from their daughter's point of view, to empathize with her aspirations. Now you may say that in those benighted days it was almost impossible for a female to become a doctor so that the parents are not to be blamed for their response to what their daughter says. But not so fast! Wouldn't it have been more respectful, more empathic with her actual aspiration, if the parents or one of them had been willing to recognize the reality of the daughter's ambition and sympathize with it? Wouldn't it have been more respectful if one or both of them had instead said: you are a very talented girl and you could make a very good doctor, but these days it is extremely difficult for a female to go to medical school much less be qualified as a medical doctor; so, unfortunately, it would make sense for you to consider some alternatives.

Consider another example, this time of cognitive or intellectual disrespect. Someone comes up with an argument against a view you have defended and tells you as much. You refuse to hear it and brush the person aside. Clearly, you are being closed-minded and intellectually disrespectful to the, say, colleague who wants you to consider some problem with your view. You are also showing an unwillingness to consider things from a perspective different from your own, and that constitutes a lack of empathy for another person's point of view. On the other side, the academic who is willing to listen to the criticisms of a colleague shows empathic respect for that colleague, and this has led me to suppose that within a sentimentalist moral philosophy respect can be unpacked in terms of empathy. Respect is an important notion for morality and moral philosophy, and in great part thanks to Immanuel Kant, we know and appreciate that. But it is perhaps also true that Kant's and Kantian accounts of respect fall short and that sentimentalism, surprisingly enough, offers us a better take on what respect amounts to.

To conclude this chapter, I would like to now show you how the notion of respect plays out in relation to larger notions of social justice. Denying people their democratic rights, denying them the right to vote for their leaders, amount to disrespect for the people of a given country. It also represents a failure or absence of social justice, and I want to show you now how care ethics can lead us to these conclusions.

To do all this, I need to bring in some work in the field of psychology. In his classic *Motivation and Personality*, A. H. Maslow argued that there are basic human needs or instincts that are to some extent independent of "lower" purely physiological desires and that among these are the need to belong, the need to be loved, and the need for the esteem of others. (There are other important aspects of his views that aren't relevant to the present discussion.) It is the last of these that I would like to apply to the political context. Our strong basic need for esteem powers an impetus toward democracy, and where rulers refuse to consider granting civil liberties or the right to vote, this can reflect a sheer desire to retain autocratic power and also express disrespect toward the ruled.

Rulers can offer pretexts for retaining autocratic rule and often say such things as: the people aren't really ready for democracy. And those who are clamoring for more democracy and greater civil liberties can naturally feel insulted by what they are being told. For example, during the failed "umbrella revolution" that occurred in Hong Kong in 2014 (I was actually there when this took place), this was precisely what was said by the Chinese Communist Party (CCP) to those who were protesting its encroachment on their accustomed freedoms and seeking greater democratization for Hong Kong. In the words of Anson Chan, the Chief Secretary of the Hong Kong government both before and after the city returned to mainland Chinese sovereignty in 1997: "Hong Kong people are outraged by this insult to their intelligence." And, I believe, they had every right to be. The CCP was expressing a kind of disdain for the people of Hong Kong that amounts to a form of disrespect.

This then connects obviously and deeply with what a sentimentalist care ethics wants to say about social justice. On analogy with what the disrespectful parents say to the daughter who aspires to become a doctor, the rulers of China didn't care enough about the people of Hong Kong to even try to understand things from their point of view. They simply brushed that viewpoint aside or paid no serious moral attention to it, and so we can say that their attitudes and behavior manifested a lack of empathic concern for the citizens of Hong Kong. If it was wrong and disrespectful for the parents to brush aside their daughter's aspirations, then it is also wrong and disrespectful for the CCP to do the same toward the people of Hong Kong, though because the wrong occurs at the socio-political level, our sentimentalism can characterize it as an injustice toward those people.

Democracy can be supported and defended in sentimentalist terms, and even though that is an unfamiliar way to do that, this kind of approach gets things right and has more plausible implications than an autonomy-emphasizing Kantian political approach that in effect tells us that magistrates shouldn't put retraining orders in place before the husband to be restrained has had his later day in court. (By then, we know, it may all be too late.) It should also be clear that the very important notion of respect can be unpacked in sentimentalist terms that avoid the problems we have found with the Kantian understanding of respect for people. But having said as much, I want now to proceed to another and I think deeper level of moral/political analysis—by bringing in (surprisingly enough) Chinese categories and concepts.

Chapter 6

Chinese Thought and Sentimentalism

The order of concepts in the title of this chapter is no accident. I think Chinese thought not only is relevant to our understanding and defense of moral sentimentalism but also provides us with a deeper and more universal basis for it. As I said at the end of the previous chapter, this is surprising; and it surprised me when I recognized or thought I recognized the deeper basis of ethics in Chinese categories. So let me explain to you why I think this.

As I mentioned in the earlier discussion of the ancient sentimentalism of Mencius, early Confucian philosophy emphasized benevolence as a virtue, but didn't have the notion of empathy that provides a contemporary basis for moral sentimentalism. However, Chinese ideas about benevolence and virtue more generally will not be the entry point of what I want to say by way of undergirding present-day sentimentalism with Chinese categories. The categories I believe can serve us in this way are yin and yang.

Perhaps the most familiar way of understanding yin and yang and their relationship treats them as opposed or contrary physical properties: yin as dark, wet, and cold and yang as, respectively, bright, dry, and warm. These contrary properties are then supposed to alternate with one another with each one driving out the other. Thus as things become darker, brightness eventually causes the darkness to vanish, and brightness is then driven out by darkness in due course. This sort of alternation was or has been supposed to explain why days follows night and night day, but such thinking is incompatible, of course, with modern-day scientific explanations of why day and night alternate (wherever they do). For that reason, the oppositional view of yin and yang and of yin/yang as the relationship between them has long been rejected for philosophical use by Chinese thinkers.

Another major tradition of yin/yang thinking sees yin and yang as complementary rather than as contraries, and this is the tradition I shall be drawing on here. Chinese thought, for example, saw Earth as yin and Heaven as yang but saw them as potentially working together rather than as in any way opposites or contraries. To do philosophical and ethical work for us, the complementarian tradition of yin and yang has to be philosophically refined and made in a sense more abstract so that it no longer involves any supposition that yin and yang are the best way to explain the occurrence of natural phenomena. One way to do that is to think of yin as receptivity and of yang as directed active purpose. But for these factors or concepts to function respectively as yin and yang, they have to be shown to depend on one another in a "friendly" non-oppositional way, something that I believe can be comfortably accomplished.

We can find an example of the interpenetration or necessary mutual dependence of yin receptivity and yang directed purpose in the phenomenon of curiosity. The curious person wants to take in facts about some part or all of the world, and that amounts to cognitive receptivity. But by the same token the curious person focuses or pays attention to some part of their environment, and although this is usually non-self-conscious, such focusing or paying of attention involves the directed purpose of knowing. Focusing is a mental *action*, and the two aspects of curiosity, if you think about it, are absolutely inseparable. Let us turn now to ethics and our notions of moral virtue because something similar turns out to be true in that realm.

I first saw the relevance of yin and yang to ethics through theorizing about the nature of compassion. I assume you will grant that the compassionate person acts out of empathy with the distress or suffering of another person (or animal), and that means there are two psychological elements in compassion: empathy with another and motivation to help them. Now a person who wants to help might be killed or injured before they are actually able to help, but at the very least compassion involves an altruistic helping *motive*. Psychologists tend to assume these two elements are only contingently related, but there is, I think, reason to believe otherwise.

Consider a father who is empathically infected (as we say) by his daughter's enthusiasm for stamp collecting. This involves more than just some undifferentiated positive feeling of enthusiasm on the part of the father but ipso facto involves him in feeling enthusiastic *about stamp collecting.* Full-bodied empathy involves taking in positive or negative feeling as directed toward some object of that feeling. By the same token, then, if someone is distressed at or by the sharp pain they have in their arm, empathy with their suffering involves being distressed *at or by that very pain, their pain.* But think what this means. To be distressed by something is to wish it diminished or eliminated altogether, and the person distressed by pain in their arm by definition wants that pain to lessen or go away. So if the empathic observer feels distress at the same pain, they too want to see it lessen or go away; and that represents motivation, altruistic motivation, to help relieve the other person's distress by doing away with or lessening the pain they feel in their arm. Therefore, the two components of compassion are not contingently related, as is so widely supposed, but, rather, the first empathic component necessarily and on purely conceptual grounds entails the altruistic motivation that is the hallmark of compassion.

But not just that. If we consider the altruism involved in compassion, we see that it and the compassion are unthinkable in the absence of any empathy with the sufferer: unthinkable as based in, say, a sense of duty. So the two components of compassion are in a tight two-way connection, and this should remind you of what I said above about yin and yang because the empathy component embodies receptivity and the necessarily related yang altruistic component embodies directed active purpose. Compassion can be thought of, then, as a yin/yang phenomenon, and once we are aware of the categories of yin and yang as conceptualized as we are conceptualizing them here, we can find a host of other mental or psychological phenomena that fall under those concepts. Let me offer you one more example.

Imagine a man who is sitting in his house and reading when he smells smoke. On investigating, he finds that his house is on fire and that the fire is fast approaching the room he is in. Recognizing the danger this represents to him, he flees out of the house out of the only door available for that purpose. If he doesn't flee, that can only be because he doesn't really or fully recognize the danger he faces of a highly painful death, and that means that if he is fully yin receptive to what is happening and its implications for himself, he will be yang purposefully motivated to leave his house via the only available door. Similarly, the fearful yang motive of fleeing can only occur if there is a yin understanding of the dangers of his situation, so the case involves yin and yang in mutual necessitation. Now we think that a compassionate person or action is morally virtuous, but what the man facing a fire exhibits is not moral virtue so much as practical rationality or reasonableness.

Further, and this is important, the applicability of yin and yang to virtuous compassion and fire-fleeing practical rationality helps explain what is valuable about them. Receptivity (as opposed to sheer passivity) is a trait or disposition we think well of, and directed purpose is surely of greater value than purely random, disorderly, or chaotic behavior. If the two cannot be separated, then they constitute a unity of good things, and we think a unity of valuable things/factors has a value independently of the value that can be attributed to those factors/things when they are considered separately. We can say, then, that yin and yang and yin/yang may represent the source of the moral value we attribute to compassion (and related qualities of character) and the rational value we attribute to self-protective action. There is a difference here in the kind of value attributed in these two kinds of cases because we think of morally valuable traits as ones that tend to help others, whereas practical reason or rationality is mainly (though far from exclusively) a matter of traits helpful to oneself. But in either case we can say that yin and yang can be thought of as underlying and helping to explain the moral and rational virtues that care ethics conceptualizes in sentimentalist terms.

But why should we want or need to bring in yin and yang as I just have. Why can't the sentimentalist rest on or with more familiar categories and factors without appealing to these foreign concepts. It is no accident that there is no standard translation of "yin" and "yang" into English. These notions characterize Far Eastern thought insofar as it derives from the Chinese, but India and the West lack them altogether, and it still may not be clear to the reader why I am treating them as so philosophically helpful. In a nutshell—and I propose to say much more about this in our next chapter—the basis and justification for bringing in these Chinese concepts is that in addition to relating and applying to familiar ethical ideas about what it is to be rational and what it is to be moral, they help us clarify and explain a whole host of philosophical issues that *surround* the questions ethics pursues on its own.

Philosophers seek to understand morality and rationality, and that is very important to many or most of them. But most philosophers have philosophical interests that lie beyond ethics narrowly or conventionally conceived, and philosophy itself, of course, contains disciplinary areas outside ethics proper. Philosophers are interested in the nature and process of knowing things about the world, and this area is called epistemology or theory of knowledge. They are interested in the nature of mathematical and logical truth and how these differ from ordinary knowledge of the world around us. They are interested in understanding aesthetic beauty or excellence in both art and nature. They are interested in exploring the nature of scientific thought and the reasons for its success. And finally, for present purposes, they are interested in the nature of the mind and of psychological functioning.

The last of these is of especial interest to most ethicists because right and wrong action are anchored in human psychology, and there are issues about human psychology that philosophers (more than psychologists) find perplexing and/or worth studying. Anyone who believes in and wants to explore right and wrong will have to have some sort of view about whether human beings have enough freedom of will to be responsible for doing bad, or good, things. They will typically suppose that humans are capable of altruism and conscientiousness and are thus not totally self-centered selfish beings, but the philosopher wants to know how altruism and the like get a foothold, educationally or congenitally, in the human mind. And I could go on at greater length. The point is that issues in ethics touch on and are affected by what philosophers want to or should say about a whole host of related questions, and, most importantly, that means that if a given ethical view doesn't sit well with what philosophers think we need to say on philosophical or psychological issues outside ethics—especially, issues about knowledge and the nature of the mind—it becomes at least somewhat questionable.

By the same token, however, if surrounding philosophical ideas fit well with some ethical view, that gives us reason, further reason, to be happy with that view. So if I can show you that yin and yang help illuminate issues about knowledge and the nature of the mind, that will support our use of them within ethics. Although sentimentalist ethics is perfectly capable of proceeding without considering philosophical issues outside of ethics, it can be further supported if those outside issues or considerations fit well with what one wants to say in ethics. There is reason or more reason to accept our previously explanation of sentimentalist values in yin/yang terms if we can show that such ethical yin/yang is part of a larger picture in which yin and yang help us to better picture of human knowledge and the human mind. That is what I would like to try to do in our next chapter.

Chapter 7

Ethics and Beyond

In this final chapter on normative ethics I want to make good on what I promised to do or attempt to do. I want to show you why Chinese thought in terms of yin and yang can provide care-ethical sentimentalism with an overall better philosophical foundation than is possible when care ethics is left entirely on its own as a normative moral theory. (Our earlier reference-fixing account of how we understand moral language can for present purposes be left to one side.) Let us begin with a description of how traditional Chinese thought understands the human mind.

The Chinese have never sharply distinguished between reason/cognition and emotion/feeling in the way that is typical in Western philosophical thinking. Here I have in mind not only what Chinese philosophers have held but also what is detectable on ordinary Chinese uses of language. The very widely used Chinese term "xin" is ordinarily translated as "heart-mind" rather than as "mind" because of the latter term's connotations or meaning in English—and similarly for equivalent terms in other Indo-European languages. In our languages such terms are thought to refer to thinking, reasoning, and cognition independently of any emotions/feelings the mind may also contain. But the Chinese don't believe in this sort of thing, and that is why their term "xin" is better translated as heart-mind. The Chinese think all thinking involves emotion or feeling, and other societies of the Far East share this assumption. The Japanese term "kokoro" and the Korean "maum" are also standardly translated as heart-mind rather than mind.

Now someone might say that this just means that the Far East makes use of different concepts from ours and leave it at that. But I think that would be a mistake. Our own Western terms for cognition, belief, thinking, and reasoning can apply only if there is feeling present, so it is a mistake to claim that our ways of thinking about the mind are perfectly in order in their own right. I want to claim that the difference between ourselves and the Chinese on the subject of the mind is not a matter of different concepts, but of the Chinese getting things right and our getting them wrong. But how to prove this?

In the West, beliefs about the world around us are generally thought to be independent of all feeling and emotion. We can believe something and also feel emotion *about* the belief or about other things, but it is held that the belief can stand on its own in the mind independently of any such emotion or feeling. All processes and states of a functioning mind involve believing something: reasoning, recognizing what falls under a certain category, planning for the future, criticizing some idea or view—all these demonstrably involve us in believing something or other.

But consider then what it is to believe some proposition p. It is to favor that proposition over competing or incompatible ideas, and favoring is an emotion—in this case a cognitive one. More significantly perhaps, many dictionaries define confidence as strong belief, and every philosopher grants that confidence that p involves a cognitively directed feeling. After all, we say that we *feel* confident that something is the case. But the dictionary definition puts belief *on the same scale* as confidence, understands it as involving a slightly or somewhat lesser degree of positive cognitive feeling toward some fact or proposition. In which case belief, like confidence, is inseparable from cognitive or, as philosophers say, epistemic feeling, and to complete the scale one can also point out that certitude represents an even more positive epistemic evaluation of some fact or proposition than is entailed by confidence, much less belief.

What follows is that all mental or psychological functioning involves feeling, and that suggests, or more than suggests, that even we in the West have heart-minds rather than minds. This can lead us toward yin/yang if we bring in some relevant further considerations. Take a given proposition about the world. To the extent we are being perceptually receptive to what is around us that belief can be characterized as yin. But where, then, is the yang?

Well, consider what it is to believe, say, that one is seeing a black swan for the first time. One has previously believed and heard that all swans are white, but here one is perceptually encountering an exception. But despite the exception one continues to believe all swans are white while at the same time recognizing that one is now confronting a black swan. Is such a thing possible? Arguably not, and that is because to believe a proposition is automatically to be disposed to make relevant inferences on the basis of that belief. But everyone agrees that inferring is an act of the mind—though as with focusing one is not usually aware that one is doing so. And in this case the inferring goes in a particular direction, toward the view that one or everyone has been mistaken to think all swans are white. Such directed active inferring clearly, then, exemplifies yang, and so all belief turns out to involve not only emotion/feeling but also yin/yang.

In the case where one yin receptively takes in the surprising fact that there are black swans, one's belief is cognitively or epistemically rational or reasonable; and the cognitive disposition to make use of what one believes to correct a previous assumption is also rational. So ordinary perceptual learning about the world around one is typically rational, and we can conceptualize that epistemic rationality in terms of yin and yang. In the case of the man faced with an oncoming fire, the yin/yang entails or amounts to a kind of practical rationality, rationality in overt actions. In the case of the person encountering a black swan, the yin/yang amounts to a kind of epistemic rationality, and the value or yin and yang can explain and justify the value we place on both epistemic and practical rationality. We are thus well beyond the area of morality. Care ethics offers us an account of moral virtue and moral rightness and wrongness, but if we undergird them with yin/yang considerations, we are doing so in a way that makes deep contract with other areas of our values: with the cognitively and with the practically rational. So yin/yang theorizing can give us a broader picture of our values than care ethics can formulate on its own, and the picture is also a philosophically deeper one because the yin/yang explains the value we place on moral virtues like compassion or benevolence that lie at the heart of care-ethical thinking. But we can go somewhat further.

Belief in a functioning mind or heart-mind involves both yin and yang, and the rationality of such belief can be explained accordingly. But what about cases where the mind isn't functional, isn't functioning well? What can we say about them? Well, imagine that someone is so upset that they cannot think straight. They are not really receptive, then, to the facts of their situation and are also too disturbed to act in any kind of concerted fashion. Clearly, they are neither epistemically nor practically rational, but these conclusions can be explained by the fact that neither desirable yin receptivity nor desirable yang directedness of purpose is present in their thinking. So irrationality can be explained in terms of the absence of value when neither yin nor yang is present, and more particularly for moral cases the moral criticizability of indifference to the plight of others can also be criticized in yin/yang terms. If a person lacks empathy for others, they will be indifferent to their fate, but they also lack an important form of human cognitive yin receptivity in a way that we considerable morally undesirable. Their lack of interest in helping those who need help will then count as morally undesirable because of the absence of directed yang motivation that indifference amounts to.

I believe that every aspect of the functioning mind or heart-mind involves yin/yang and that every aspect of a dysfunctional mind shows an absence of both yin and yang. For example, a state of blind panic or of utter mental depression involves neither receptivity nor directed active purposiveness, and a general yin/yang account can explain why these states are dysfunctional and also irrational. Again, but in larger terms, yin/yang allows us to place morality in a wider and deeper philosophically explanatory and justificatory context, so, finally, I want to suggest that care ethicists take yin and yang on board in the way they deploy and develop their approach to normative morality. Ethics takes in a wide variety of issues and subject matters, but it is only one part of philosophy, and all of us ethicists need to remember that.

Chapter 8

Some Thoughts about Metaethics and Applied Ethics

I indicated at the start that this book would be primarily concerned with introducing you to normative ethics. Normative ethics is and has almost always been the center of ethical inquiry among philosophers, but I also indicated that both metaethics and applied ethics are normally classified under or within the field of ethics. I am going to say something briefly about each of these in this final chapter, starting with metaethics.

The chief focus of metaethics is on questions about the meaning of moral terminology, and I have previously referred you to different theories of moral semantics. I largely gave those theories short shrift because most of them and starting with David Hume insist on the non-objectivity of moral statements and judgments; and I have mentioned some reasons to hope and think otherwise. However, in the list of relevant readings that follows the main text of this book, I shall include a book edited by S. Darwall, A. Gibbard, and P. Railton that offers relevant contemporary discussions of metaethics.

I want to say a bit more about applied ethics. Applied ethics deals with present-day moral issues concerning abortion, euthanasia (mercy killing), world hunger, capital punishment, the rights of LGBTQ+ individuals, and of course the list could go on. Quite typically those who address such issues do so in the light of one or another normative ethical theory. Given that virtue ethics has only become influential in recent decades, this has meant that most philosophers and others who have previously addressed issues in applied ethics have done so from either a utilitarian or a Kantian point of view. However, given the increased academic influence of virtue ethics, such questions are now frequently addressed in virtue-ethical terms, and even care ethics, which came along somewhat later, has begun to have many applied-ethical practitioners.

However, it is also possible to address problems in applied ethics without having any theoretical ethical commitment, and this is something that occurs very frequently. Those who proceed in this way assume they can rely on our ordinary pre-theoretical moral intuitions plus thorough research into relevant facts when they seek to offer solutions to present-day practical or applied moral problems. But of course many of those problems bring up considerations on both sides of any given proposed solution, so the common-sense approach to applied ethical issues often has to rely on the delicate intuitive balancing and weighing of relevant factors, and naturally enough there are often disagreements about how to balance and how much to weigh one or another relevant moral factor.

However, that doesn't mean that Kantian and utilitarian ventures in applied ethics are spared such complex considerations. Kantians typically agree that how well an action comports with one or another version of the categorical imperative can be a very delicate and complex matter, and the utilitarians always grant that application of the principle of utility, which says we ought to perform the action that will have comparatively best consequences for human happiness, requires a relevant knowledge of facts, facts about what is likely to cause what, if one is to decide in utilitarian terms which solution to any current moral problem is supported by the principle of utility.

To that extent, applied ethics is just as complicated as normative ethics, but there is a major difference in how philosophically deep each goes. The applied ethicist relies on common-sense intuitions or on one or another normative theory that they don't seek to defend in any extended way—whereas normative ethics can and does criticize so-called common sense or ordinary moral thinking, and, perhaps more significantly, it typically seeks to understand *why* the things we think are wrong are wrong and *why* the things we think are right or morally acceptable are that way. This means, as I have indicated, going philosophically and ethically deeper than applied ethics seeks to go, and I dare say that is one reason why philosophers generally have a higher opinion of normative ethics than of applied ethics. And, of course, this book represents one way of giving expression to such an attitude. Readers will have to judge for themselves whether my emphasis on the normative gives them the most important things they want or would want to know about ethics. I leave the matter to all of you.

Conclusion

This book is the only introduction to ethics that gives rationalism and sentimentalism equal hearings. It also differs from other introductions in the way it brings Chinese thinking and Chinese concepts into a discussion of ethics that takes off from and mainly focuses on issues and theories in Western philosophy. I have, further, pushed Chinese ideas as qualifying and deepening Western thinking not only about the ethical but about philosophy more generally. That counts, in the sense mentioned in the Introduction, as an example of doing "world philosophy." This is an increasingly internationalized world we live in, but most philosophers and ethicists have confined their interest and their thinking to only one of the world's main philosophical traditions. It is my hope, though, that this will change, and the effort here to show the ways in which world philosophy can do plausible and promising new philosophical work is supposed to illustrate for readers with no philosophy background how and why such a possibility makes sense. In other work I have sought to make these points in greater detail to and for academic philosophers both East and West, and I look forward to a day in which more and more philosophers are willing and able to work in a world-philosophical manner.

Further Reading

The following list of readings contains bibliographical references to the most important texts we have discussed.

Aristotle, *Nicomachean Ethics*, any modern edition.

Bentham, J., *An Introduction to the Principles of Morals and Legislation*, Methuen, 1982.

Cummiskey, D., *Kantian Consequentialism*, Oxford, 1995.

Confucius, *Analects*, any edition.

Darwall, S., *The Second-Person Standpoint*, Harvard, 2006.

Darwall, S. et al., *Moral Discourse and Practice*, Oxford, 1997.

Dworkin, R., *Taking Rights Seriously*, Duckworth, 1978.

Gilligan, C., *In a Different Voice*, Harvard, 1982.

Hume, D., *A Treatise of Human Nature*, any edition.

Kant, I., *Groundwork (or Fundamental Principles) of the Metaphysics of Morals*, any edition.

Kripke, S., *Naming and Necessity*, Blackwell, 1980.

Maslow, A., *Motivation and Personality,* Harper and Row, 1954.

Mencius, *The Mencius*, any edition.

Nagel, T., *The Possibility of Altruism*, Oxford, 1970.

Rawls, J., *A Theory of Justice*, Harvard, 1971.

Scanlon, T., *What We Owe to Each Other*, Harvard, 1998.

Sidgwick, H., *The Methods of Ethics*, 7th edition, Macmillan, 1907.

Slote, M., *Moral Sentimentalism*, Oxford University Press, 2010.

Pay a visit to:

Quick Immersion Series

Visit our WEB:
https://www.quickimmersions.com/

You will get:

+Information of all published books

+News of the books in preparation

+You can subscribe to "A Quick Immersion"

+Links to other spaces of our WEB

+Contact us

+Receive timely information on all our titles

Printed in Great Britain
by Amazon